# The Divine Mrs S

April De Angelis's plays include *Infamous* (Jermyn Street Theatre), *Kerry Jackson* (National Theatre), *My Brilliant Friend* (adapted from Elena Ferrante's novels for Rose Theatre, Kingston, and NT), *House Party* (BBC Four and Headlong Theatre), *Gin Craze!*, a musical with Lucy Rivers (Royal & Derngate), *Extinct* (Stratford East), *Rune* (New Vic Theatre, Newcastle-under-Lyme), *The Village* (Stratford East), *Wild East* (Royal Court), *A Laughing Matter* (Out of Joint/NT/tour), *The Warwickshire Testimony* (RSC), *The Positive Hour* (Out of Joint/Hampstead/Old Vic; Sphinx), *Headstrong* (NT Shell Connections), *Playhouse Creatures* (Sphinx Theatre Company), *Hush* (Royal Court), *Soft Vengeance* (Graeae Theatre Company), *The Life and Times of Fanny Hill* (adapted from the James Cleland novel), *Ironmistress* (ReSisters Theatre Company), *Wuthering Heights* (adapted from Emily Brontë's novel for Birmingham Rep), *Jumpy* (Royal Court and Duke of York's Theatres), *Gastronauts* (Royal Court) and *After Electra* (Theatre Royal, Plymouth). Her work for BBC Radio includes *Visitants*, *The Outlander*, which won the Writers' Guild Award 1992, and *Cash Cows* for the *Woman's Hour* serial. For opera: *Flight* with composer Jonathan Dove (Glyndebourne), and the libretto for *Silent Twins* (Almeida).

T0323173

APRIL DE ANGELIS

# The Divine Mrs S

faber

First published in 2024
by Faber and Faber Limited
The Bindery, 51 Hatton Garden,
London, EC1N 8HN

Typeset by Brighton Gray
Printed and bound in the UK by CPI Group (Ltd), Croydon CR0 4YY

A CIP record for this book
is available from the British Library

ISBN 978-0-571-39193-6

2 4 6 8 10 9 7 5 3 1

The Divine Mrs S was first performed at Hampstead Theatre, London, on 22 March 2024. The cast was as follows:

**Patti** Anushka Chakravarti
**Clara/Joanna Baillie/Galindo/Arthur** Eva Feiler
**Kemble** Dominic Rowan
**Mrs Larpent/Cowslip/Turnkey** Sadie Shimmin
**Boaden/Thomas Lawrence/Percy Scraggs/Charles** Gareth Snook
**Sarah Siddons** Rachael Stirling

*Director* Anna Mackmin
*Designer* Lez Brotherston
*Lighting Designer* Mark Henderson
*Composer and Sound Designer* Max Pappenheim

The Divine Mrs S is a Hampstead Theatre/AKO Foundation Next Decade commission.

With thanks to Anna Mackmin

# Characters

**Sarah Siddons,** an actress
**Kemble,** her brother
**Patti,** her young companion
**Mrs Larpent,** the censor's wife
**Mr Boaden,** a theatre critic
**Thomas Lawrence,** an artist
**Clara,** a young mother
**Cowslip,** a comic actress
**Joanna Baillie,** a playwright
**Galindo,** a fencing master
**Percy Scraggs,** an actor
**Turnkey,** a woman worker in a madhouse
**Charles** *and* **Arthur,** actors

# THE DIVINE MRS S

## Notes

All except Siddons, Patti and Kemble double or triple.

This is to be embraced in a theatrical style.

The main setting is the dressing room of Mrs Siddons.

Other settings – the stage itself, the madhouse – should feel like they are taking place in the 'onstage' space.

# Part One

## ONE

*Onstage.*
  *The last moments of the last scene of* The Stranger *by Kotzebue.*
  *Kemble and Siddons as estranged husband and wife.*
  *The whole scene is interspersed with emotional groans, sighs, sobbing from audience.*

**Kemble** (*as Stranger*) For it is I! Your estranged husband that you see before you!

**Siddons** (*as Mrs Halle*) My husband?

**Kemble** (*as Stranger*) Disguised as this stranger.

**Siddons** (*as Mrs Halle*) My husband! Oh feel for my mother's heart, are my children still alive?

**Kemble** (*as Stranger*) Yes they are alive.

**Siddons** (*as Mrs Halle*) And well?

**Kemble** (*as Stranger*) Yes they are well.

**Siddons** (*as Mrs Halle*) Heaven be praised. William must be much grown.
  And Little Amelia, is she not still your favourite? For eight long years I have laboured for the poor and not seen my dear ones. Oh let me behold them once again? Let me once more kiss the features of their father in his babes and I will kneel to you and part with them forever!

**Kemble** (*as Stranger*) Willingly, Adelaide. This very night. I expect the children every minute. I have already sent my servant for them. I pledge my word to send them to the castle as soon as they arrive. There if you please they may remain till daybreak tomorrow. Then they must go with me.

**Siddons** (*as Mrs Halle*) In this world then we have no more to say. Forget an adulterous wretch who will never forget you. And when my penance shall have broken my heart we will meet again in a better world.

*She goes to leave.*

**Kemble** (*as Stranger*) Adelaide Halle – stay – you may be mine again.

**Siddons** (*as Mrs Halle*) OH!

*She faux-faints.*

**Children's Voices** Mama! Mama!

**Siddons** (*as Mrs Halle*) My children!

*Siddons stretches her arms out as if to her children.*
*She faints for real.*
*End of play.*
*Big audience response. Cries of 'Siddons!'*
*Kemble takes his bow.*
*Siddons seems unable to get up.*

**Kemble** Get up, sister. Get up!

*He helps her up.*
*She is carried off.*

Is it too much to ask for the theatrics to be kept on the stage? Careful of the costume! Donated by the Duchess of Devonshire.

**Charles** She did it excellently well though, Mr Kemble. Not a dry eye in the house.

**Kemble** The first half of the play I may confidently assert was mine. At this rate I may be forced to amend her

4

contract to 'actress must be able to exit under her own steam'.

Let's hope this is not an affectation she will continue to indulge. She's a dead weight.

TWO

*Backstage, Drury Lane Theatre, 1800.*
*Siddons lays on her couch, unmoving.*

**Kemble** (*addressing Patti*) When she comes offstage she is insensible. She lays on the couch there. You mustn't force her out of her distraction but wait for nature to bring her out. You may administer a glass of water. Don't fling it on her though the temptation might be strong. She may become voluble. Do not contradict her. Don't offer any advice – indeed that would be best as you are experiencing that portion of youth which has not yet furnished you with the prerequisite disappointment and failure. She may speak of death. Of money. Of her faithless husband. Of money. Of her children. Of money. Of the contemporary dearth of new writing. Of her image, her fear of scandal. Of her brother, me. Of money. Help her out of her stage clothes and into her own. She tends to sit a while in contemplation as she takes off her make-up. What luxury! She may still have the vestiges of the character clinging to her – she may speak their words –

**Siddons** (*moans*) Ah my children.

**Kemble** It should wear off as she eats a little light supper. Don't freak out like the last three girls she's had. You're old theatre stock, you should be used to it.

You will be fine as long as you bring no problems.

**Patti** I will try not to.

**Kemble** Trying is absolutely not good enough.

**Patti** I will not. I will try to will not.

**Kemble** Trying is underachieving.

**Patti** I suppose it is. I won't try in a good way.

**Kemble** Are you literate?

**Patti** Normally.

**Kemble** The public has taken Siddons to their hearts extravagantly. That means she pays the wages of every poor soul that has the misfortune to work here. If you let her down you let down not just the acting company, the dressers, the backstage crew, the prompters and the wigsters but worst of all me.

**Patti** That's quite a lot. Should I curtsy?

**Kemble** Anything that works. Try to cheer her. You take it from here. Oh and hide the cheese knife.

*He exits.*
*A groan from Siddons.*

**Siddons** Do not mix the rouge with the white.

**Patti** Is that the play?

**Siddons** No.

**Patti** Oh I won't.

**Siddons** No more to say.

**Patti** All right.

**Siddons** That is the play.

**Patti** Patti Wilkinson. I was sent for. You once worked for my father's company in Barnsley.

**Siddons** How old?

**Patti** Eighteen.

**Siddons**  Same as my Maria. She was snatched from me. An angel. Bring me wine.

*Patti passes it to her. She drinks.*

Soon I won't be able to feel my extremities.

**Patti**  Oh dear.

**Siddons**  That is to be desired. No one wants the extremes, Patti, unless they're safely onstage. Lately I have found them impossible to bear even there.

**Patti**  Eighty-seven fainters tonight.

**Siddons**  Including me.
 Poor darling Maria floats before my eyes. I wear her portrait.

*Shows Patti her locket with portrait.*

**Patti**  So pretty.

**Siddons**  She had a two-octave range. A grieving mother and they force me to play a grieving mother.

**Patti**  Who does?

**Siddons**  The audience.

**Patti**  They wouldn't if they saw how much it upsets you.

**Siddons**  An innocent. When I play distressed mothers the haters are sated.

**Patti**  No one hates you, you're Siddons.

**Siddons**  You should see the letters.
 Poisonous missives! They circulate them in the coffee houses. Accusing me of neglecting my dead child. Putting my work first. Calling me a money-grubbing – I'll spare you the details, dear. I was hissed giving my Volumnia.

**Patti**  Oh no.

**Siddons** I have no ambition for myself. I earn the money which puts bread on the table. Should I let my children starve? And now my poor Sally is ailing – Dr Richards isn't cheap – ten shillings a visit and they wish to slay my honour.

**Patti** Father says you are a devoted mother. You gave birth onstage.

**Siddons** In the wings, Patti love, there is a difference.

**Patti** Mum always says audiences love two things equally: cheering and booing.

**Siddons** How wretched is she who depends upon the instability of public favour.

**Patti** Here's your supper.

*Patti picks up the tray to give to Siddons, spies the cheese knife. She surreptitiously hides it. Siddons spots this.*

**Siddons** Am I expected to swallow the cheese whole? You're a spy!

**Patti** No. Mr Kemble said –

**Siddons** Mr Kemble!

**Patti** He's worried that you might –

**Siddons** With a cheese knife? Allow me some dignity. Just as I was beginning to like you!

**Patti** I didn't mean you any harm by it.

**Siddons** Look like the innocent flower but be the serpent under it! Your tenure is at an end.

**Patti** Oh no. Please give me another chance. I've been looking forward to this more than anything. I'd feel disgraced to be sent straight home. I've only been here ten minutes.

**Siddons**  You should consider the stage, Patti.

**Patti**  I was about to be betrothed and I wasn't sure and
father said well you need to go away and think about it for
a bit. It's a big decision you may not want to be
a missionary with Dicky Suet going bothering people in
India. He's an actor who's found Jesus. This came up and
Dad said it might just be the thing. See a bit of theatre life.

*Pause.*

**Siddons**  You certainly would have seen a bit of theatre life,
me. But now I'm afraid it's Dicky Suet for you.

**Patti**  I'll go then.
Father says you are the best actress he ever saw. And
I think so too. Goodbye and I'm very sorry.

**Siddons**  Well. Perhaps I've been a little hasty. You've come
to the right place, Patti, and if it helps you learn anything
I'll be glad of it.
There are some people you must never let into this room.
There's a list but top is Mr Thomas Lawrence, artist.
Grossly ungrateful. I made him. Never, never let him in.
Have I your word on that?

**Patti**  Yes.

**Siddons**  Then we will rub along.

**Patti**  What will I do if he tries to come in?

**Siddons**  You will stop him.

**Patti**  How?

**Siddons**  You'll think of something otherwise what use are
you to me? You will be on the first coach heading back to
Barnsley.

*Enter Kemble.*

**Patti**  Are you on the list, sir?

**Kemble** Behave. Sister? Are you yourself?

**Siddons** Apparently.

**Kemble** Marvellous. The last thing I need is my leading lady off.

**Siddons** I don't faint to cause you trouble.

**Kemble** I know that. I'm the manager. Why would you wish to make my life more difficult? Like everyone else you're terrifically grateful I took this place on. What a mess. The first time I looked at the books I almost vomited. They were illegible and covered in anchovies. I thought, who's been keeping the damn things, Falstaff? You can be the carefree artist. I have to muddy my talent with business. And now this new 'condition' of yours. At each exit I said to myself will she be gracing us with her presence again tonight? Who knows? I'm good but there's a limit to anyone's improvisational capacity.

**Siddons** Did it cross your mind that I would find the part a trifle trying with Maria a fortnight dead?

**Kemble** I didn't know she was going to die did I?

**Siddons** Highly inconvenient. As long as you get to strut the stage in a quilted waistcoat you're quite content for me to be prostrate?

**Kemble** You soak up the applause quick enough.

**Siddons** So would you if you got it.

**Kemble** *The Stranger* opened to superb reviews, plays to packed houses and isn't going anywhere.

**Siddons** It's as if my limbs fill with lead and my mind is screaming.

**Kemble** Could be your age? You're approaching your grand climacteric.

**Siddons**  My God I'm barely forty . . . two.
I can still play young marrieds.

**Kemble**  Just. Think of the box office, that usually gets you through.

**Siddons**  I have dependants, five – four children and one husband, a perpetually resting actor.

**Kemble**  At least Adelaide Halle is a bit interesting, she commits adultery.

**Siddons**  She didn't even have the gumption to conceal the matter.

**Kemble**  We don't always get to choose our parts. In art as in life.

**Siddons**  I'm happy to partner you in finding a new play, brother.

**Kemble**  No! The last thing I need is an argument every morning.

**Siddons**  I've exhausted my tolerance for the saintly wounded brigade.

**Kemble**  Once a manager gives in to one actress, the rest would be on him like a pack of hyenas.

**Siddons**  You see, Patti. All the sensitivity of a shoe buckle.

**Kemble**  I'm not insensitive – you can alternate her with Calista in *The Fair Penitent.*

**Siddons**  Same part, different bonnet.

**Kemble**  God you're difficult.

*He opens the door to leave, sees Mrs Larpent approaching.*

Damn, it's her. Larpent, the censor, his wife.

**Siddons** (*to Patti*) She has the job, he has the title. Never say that out loud, Patti.

**Patti** No.

**Kemble** She pursues me. Hard enough running this bloody place without the ministrations of that creature of darkness. Total harpy.

*Mrs Larpent enters.*

Mrs Larpent, how wonderful.

**Siddons** My dear Anna.

**Mrs Larpent** Siddons. You were unsurpassable. Magnificent! The sudden changes wrought within a sentence from animated hope and surprise to disappointment, depression and then utter contempt is beyond any power but yours. You will shine down the centuries. You were quite good too, Kemble.

**Kemble** Yes. I was trying something new tonight. A cataract in the left eye. Perhaps you noticed?

**Mrs Larpent** No. I come with bad news. There is a problem.

**Kemble** We've had an issue with one of the child actors – off with rickets.

**Mrs Larpent** Rather more serious than that I'm afraid. Acting in women revolts against female delicacy. But you have changed all that, transformed the British theatre single-handedly into a place of decency. You are Siddons, our other queen. Siddons the faithful mother. I do not wish to see you as Mrs Halle, an adulteress.

**Siddons** I would never have consented to play a serial offender. She made one mistake, his name was Aubrey.

**Kemble** To be fair the husband dabbled too.

**Mrs Larpent** Unlike man the stain upon woman is ineradicable.

What appeared tolerable on the page now appears intolerable on the stage.

Isabella in *The Fatal Marriage* accidentally became a bigamist but Mrs Halle is a different matter. She was fully conscious during the hateful episode.

**Kemble** I receive the box office receipts every night and I would like to make the case for infidelity. We do need to keep our doors open. You understand that much of our business at least?

**Mrs Larpent** And more. There's not a play in the land that has not brushed my bureau but this one is dangerous and must be stopped.

**Kemble** Stopped!?

**Mrs Larpent** The theatre should be girding our loins against invasion not lubricating them with adultery. Since the revolution, French women are queueing up for divorce. If the family falls apart the nation follows. That's how they ended up with Napoleon, a very short killer. He could be here in six weeks, living in St James's Palace, raping and pillaging.

**Kemble** He's a theatre man apparently.

**Mrs Larpent** The licence to perform should never have been granted. I revoke it.

**Kemble** You can't do that. We've invested in the backdrops. *The Stranger* is earning us a small fortune. Do you know how rare that is – the words 'Play' and 'Money' in the same sentence? Say something, sister.

**Siddons** Anna. Your taste is impeccable. I can't oppose you.

**Kemble** Even if I offered you next Thursday as a benefit night? All the takings in your pocket.

**Mrs Larpent**  Siddons is not venal.

*Beat.*

**Siddons**  No.

**Kemble**  Come on!

**Siddons**  You always advise me, brother, that I have not the head for choosing plays. I hardly think I can go against your counsel now.

**Kemble**  You can give it a go. In fact I've been meaning to say, in reference to our recent conversation, that I can now see the sense in allowing you to select the odd play for Drury Lane.

**Siddons**  A sudden change of heart.

**Kemble**  I've realised that with your long and dedicated service to this theatre you are indeed a rare repository or something like that.

**Mrs Larpent**  Do you mean to dissuade me, Sarah?

**Siddons**  Never. I wouldn't presume. How is your daughter, Clara?

**Mrs Larpent**  Unhappily married.
  I've advised her as only a mother can. Become invisible and in that way the marriage may prosper.

**Siddons**  Perhaps if she saw this play she might find it instructive?

**Mrs Larpent**  To see you play a harlot? No indeed.

**Siddons**  To show how a woman's sacrifice heals a marriage.
  As you know, I have suffered a loss.

**Mrs Larpent**  Your dear daughter.

**Siddons**  I believe Mrs Halle has cried every night since she was last allowed to hold her children. She lives for them.

**Mrs Larpent** Except for the time she . . .

**Siddons** For which she repents by working as a housekeeper for eight years.

**Mrs Larpent** That's a lot of folding.

**Siddons** But *The Stranger* ends with *reunion*, which must surely assist our cause of national unity.

**Mrs Larpent** I just love your voice. You could say anything and I'd listen. Even rubbish.

**Siddons** And I have something for you.

**Mrs Larpent** For me?

*Siddons gets out a small parcel.*

**Siddons** A lock of my hair.

**Mrs Larpent** My dear Siddons, this is too much! I'm overcome. Thank you. Perhaps I have been looking at this the wrong way after all.

**Kemble** How delightful. Am I to assume the theatre has your assent to continue to perform a play?

**Mrs Larpent** Your sister has persuaded me.

**Kemble** Jolly good.

**Mrs Larpent** I could stay here all night chatting to you, dear Siddons, but that would be selfish when I know how you long to be at home with your dear ones.

*She exits.*

**Kemble** A lock of my hair. Not I presume from your armpit?

**Siddons** As you know I hate the damn part, brother. Never repeat that, Patti.

**Patti** I'll never repeat anything.

**Siddons** That weakling of a character, Mrs Halle, laps up her penance like a beaten dog. I'm holding you to your promise. I intend to find a new play myself, brother.

**Kemble** Good luck with that. The trouble with playwrights is they've never set foot in a theatre. They casually write 'Enter on horseback', they haven't given a bloody thought to getting a horse up the backstairs. Cleaning up its shit. Tempting it on with a carrot. They're impractical and most of them can't write dialogue.

*He leaves.*

**Siddons** (*as if reading a stage direction*) Siddons, anxious to be with her children, exits without delay.

*She doesn't. She sits down and opens a play from the stack on her desk. She hands one to Patti.*

Look for anything with big speeches for an actress.

*They begin to read.*

### THREE

**Siddons** Due to popular demand, Siddons is again playing Mrs Halle, the most provoking piece of still life one could ever have the misfortune to meet.

The Stranger *again.*

(*As Mrs Halle.*) In this world then we have no more to say. Forget an adulterous wretch who will never forget you. And when my penance shall have broken my heart we will meet again in a better world.

*She goes to leave.*

**Kemble** (*as Stranger*) Adelaide Halle – stay – you may be mine again.

**Siddons** (*as Mrs Halle*) OH!

*She faux-faints.*

**Children's Voices** Mama! Mama!

**Siddons** (*as Mrs Halle*) My children!

*Siddons stretches her arms out as if to her children.*
*She faints for real.*

**Kemble** Every time!
Fainting epidemic out there. Is this a theatre or a damn hospital? Perhaps we could make up our minds.

*Siddons is brought in, laid on couch.*

Deposit her face-up. Best thing. We wouldn't want her choking on a cushion.

**Siddons** Pass me the nun's cream.

**Patti** No, we've just had the curtain.

**Siddons** That's right.

*Kemble enters.*

**Patti** It's Mr Kemble.

**Kemble** I don't need an introduction. It's my theatre. Boaden's in. The chief theatre critic, he's coming now.

**Siddons** I've given everything. I can't possibly give any more.

*Enter Boaden, Siddons gets up.*

(*Effusively.*) Mr Boaden.

**Kemble** Dear Boaden.

**Boaden** The actress like a resistless torrent has borne down all before her. The country has gone mad for her. Kemble, you must feel the chill wind of her genius, lapping at your heels.

**Kemble** Indeed my sister is a remarkable partner in the arts of Thespis.

**Boaden** She attends to other actors when they're speaking, never lapses from character. I've observed Mr Barrymore pick at his nose whilst awaiting Juliet's cue in the balcony scene.

**Kemble** Animal.

**Boaden** Although we are not in the habit of comparing men and women as it's disadvantageous to the gentler sex, for Siddons we make an exception. We must account her half-man.

**Kemble** Try being onstage with that.

**Boaden** She towers over her sex. Surpassing the feminine beautiful, touching upon the masculine sublime. The whole of wronged womanhood speaks through her voice.

**Siddons** I would protest but you critics are never wrong. We mortals merely do the acting.

**Boaden** If I am to write your life, madam, prepare to familiarise yourself with my encomiums.

**Kemble** Her *life*?

**Siddons** Yes, brother, it is an astonishing honour.

**Boaden** I will not dwell on the domestic tragedy you have recently suffered.

**Siddons** Work is my solace.

**Boaden** But trace the extraordinary highlights of your meteoric career.
    Preserving your staggering talent for posterity.

**Kemble** Do you need a whole book?

**Siddons** Patti, refreshments?

**Kemble** You'll be sharing the proceeds of the sales between you?

**Siddons** Brother, do not plash around in the details. Mr Boaden, your book shall be a welcome defence of my besieged reputation.

*Boaden gets out a notebook.*

**Boaden** Ma'am. It's a peculiar happiness that you have so little imitated other performers through a conviction you could only be great by being truly original.

**Siddons** I always study my parts with diligence and, unlike most of my fellows who don't bother, I read the play. That's hardly genius.

**Kemble** Exactly. We both owe what talents we possess to our parents, sir.

**Boaden** Travelling players?

**Kemble** Hardworking, honourable people. I made my entrance in an hotel. King George III.

**Boaden** In Basingstoke. I know it.

**Kemble** She was born in a –

**Siddons** More modest establishment –

**Kemble** The Leg of Mutton Inn, Wales.

**Siddons** Where my father was performing his Richard III. Mother had just given her Lady Anne and managed to make it upstairs before the domestic incident occurred.

**Boaden** The incident?

**Siddons** Parturition. Two days later we were on the road to St Austell for *The Winter's Tale*.

**Boaden** And so a phenomenon was born.

**Kemble**  Apparently my first word was 'boots'. My father was always shouting that at his dresser.

**Boaden**  Your Lady Macbeth –

*Siddons and Kemble react to this superstitiously and together, perhaps they turn in a circle and knock on wood.*

**Siddons**  We're a superstitious tribe. Forgive us.

**Kemble**  The theatre has a primitive heart. The first actors imitated goats. Mostly we have moved on.

**Boaden**  The Scottish Queen has become your exclusive possession. You alone have penetrated the mystery of her soul.

**Siddons**  The part is such a long way from my natural character. So full of ruthless, self-serving ambition, how could I bring her to life?

**Kemble**  Yet my sister manages to do so uncannily.

**Boaden**  A great strain for the feminine psyche.

**Siddons**  But then the answer came to me – she thinks only of her husband.

**Boaden**  Inspired!

**Siddons**  Crushing down her true woman's nature to nurture *his* ambition, naturally she pays the price for it and goes mad.

**Boaden**  In the sleepwalking scene, you departed from tradition in a most extraordinary way.

**Siddons**  It's quite simple, Mr Boaden – I just read the stage directions. It says 'Enters in a nightgown'. So I did.

**Boaden**  I believe Mrs Pritchard played it in full Tudor, ruff and farthingale.

**Siddons** I observed a somnambulist for accuracy. They were, as you might expect, in their nightclothes.

**Boaden** And yet that wasn't your greatest innovation. 'Out, damn'd spot. Will these hands ne'er be clean?'

**Siddons** She wouldn't be *holding her candle. I placed* the candle down in order to perform the phantasmatic action of washing the blood clean.

**Kemble** Sheridan had warned her against it. She wouldn't listen.

**Siddons** He feared a riot. I would have submitted but alas there was no time. And so, with an unwilling heart, I did it my way.

**Boaden** And then the audience.

**Siddons** Went mad for it.

**Boaden** The King was present and led some of the loudest applause ever heard in a theatre.

**Kemble** Barring my Titus.

**Boaden** Ah, yes that.

**Kemble** I have taken my study *beyond* the play, sir.

**Boaden** Beyond?

**Kemble** I observe its history, the manners of the time and indeed the accents. My discovery is this. We have been saying Shakespeare all wrong. Defiling the Bard's tongue.

**Siddons** He is the scholar, I was not sent to school.

**Kemble** Take the 'H' sound. Shakespeare didn't go around saying that. He said 'Aaitch'. So we should not say 'Hamlet, Prince of Denmark' but 'Ahhmlet'.

**Boaden** More like 'omelette'?

**Kemble**  Precisely.

**Boaden**  It does fall a little oddly on the ear.

**Siddons**  How can the audience be expected to understand what you are saying, brother?

**Kemble**  They will have to learn as that is how Shakespeare wished it spoken. Ahhmlet.

**Siddons**  To be or not to be, Omelette, Prince of Denmark.

**Boaden**  Your Scottish Queen, Shakespeare's prodigy of a woman, has become the most powerful of your attractions. The terror of your eye, the perfection of your voice, holds us all captive. Don't leave it too long, Melpomene, our tragic muse, until next time.

*He leaves.*

**Kemble**  So oily he's dripping.

**Siddons**  He's a dear friend. Who writes our reviews.

**Kemble**  Forgive me, sister. Tonight I had the distinct impression you were milking it.

**Siddons**  Would I ever stoop to that?

**Kemble**  Frequently. Goodnight.

*He exits.*

**Siddons**  Now I shall get changed.
Transform once more into an ordinary woman.

**Patti**  You could never be that. Dad said you played one very well.

**Siddons**  Dear Wilkinson. What did he mean?

**Patti**  You got your kids to act with you onstage. Everyone exclaimed you were the best mother in the world offstage as well as on and no one blamed you for leaving them for the theatre each night.

**Siddons**  Do send him my best love.

> *A knock at the door.*
> *Patti goes to open it.*
> *We hear a man's voice.*

**Patti**  Mrs Siddons is indisposed.

**Siddons**  Who is it?

**Thomas**  (*off*)Thomas Lawrence.

**Siddons**  Keep him out, Patti!

**Patti**  You are on the list, I'm not going back to Barnsley, sir, desist!

**Siddons**  (*shouting*) Get away you detestable freak. Away AWAY!
Let him in, Patti.

> *In bursts Thomas Lawrence with a bag of money.*
> *Siddons emerges, underdressed.*

Get out.

**Thomas**  Siddons.

**Siddons**  You monster.

**Thomas**  How is my beloved Sally?

**Siddons**  She has erased you from her consciousness.

**Thomas**  It's not possible. I cry every night.

**Siddons**  Good. So do I. And every morning. We want nothing to do with you.

**Thomas**  I ask just a single interview with my beloved girl.

**Siddons**  That would be hazardous in the extreme. You are a danger to my family.
He drove my poor Maria to an early grave.

**Thomas**  She had consumption.

**Siddons** Don't say that word, it's unlucky.

He was engaged to my Sally, changed his mind, got engaged to my Maria, changed his mind again went back again to Sally.

**Patti** Awkward.

**Thomas** I'm an artist. I'm constitutionally insatiable. I blame you for bewitching me in the first place.

**Siddons** Of course. You're a man. Patti, call for stage door. Reg Gubbins is eighty-three but he can still manage the stairs.

**Thomas** I'll never forget the first time I saw you at my father's hotel.

**Siddons** Impossible to know you were a demon in disguise.

**Thomas** You came down the stairs of the Bear Inn, my breath left my body.

**Siddons** You were only seven.

**Thomas** The most beautiful –

**Siddons** Stop –

**Thomas** – desirable –

**Siddons** No –

**Thomas** – dynamic –

**Siddons** Well –

**Thomas** – woman I was ever to lay eyes upon, never to be surpassed. I drew you then. Let me paint you again now.

**Siddons** Sally would never forgive me. All those late-night sittings – scandalous . . . she has given you up on her sister's deathbed orders. And I should entertain you?

**Thomas** I exhibited the painting I made of you as Mrs Halle – half the entrance money.

*He shows her a bag of coins.*

**Siddons**  You could have sent a servant.

**Thomas**  Two hundred quid. I don't think so.

**Siddons**  On the table.

*He puts it on the table.*

**Thomas**  I find myself temporarily in an impecunious position.

**Siddons**  Skint again are we?

**Thomas**  You're always short yourself.

**Siddons**  Throw that in my face do you, infidel, you know my husband's mistress wears my earnings on her back.

**Thomas**  My picture of Mrs Halle, I gave her liquid eyes, shame-choked cheeks, fluttering breast, tender lips. That painting was a bloody winner for us.

**Siddons**  You do have a talent for making me appear fresh. All that must be renounced.

**Thomas**  Must we always go through this tiresome act?
We need each other – like the flesh of the fruit needs the skin and the pips.

**Siddons**  What a gratuitously intimate metaphor.

**Thomas**  People flock to see my paintings. We've built Siddons between us and cashed in.

**Siddons**  Maria's dead a month. You snake, I curse you.

**Thomas**  I'm at my usual lodgings. Mornings are good. Or I could pop in after the curtain.

**Siddons**  Leave before I blast you with contagious fogs!

**Thomas**  Magnificent.

*He exits, passing Patti.*

**Patti** (*shouting down to Reg*) Reg, stand down!

**Siddons** What on earth came over you, Patti, to admit him?

*Kemble at the door.*

**Patti** She's not receiving visitors.

**Kemble** (*off*) I'm not a visitor, you little hussy, I'm the manager.

*He pauses for a beat, noticing Patti.*
*He enters.*

(*To Siddons*) One word. Touring.

**Siddons** No. I don't like dressing rooms with buckets or anywhere north of Birmingham. It doesn't suit to be away from Sally at present.

**Kemble** It's not me, it's your husband. I want you here, not on some poxy tour.

**Siddons** You should have told him that.

**Kemble** I did but apparently two years ago you invested in a whale fishery on the coast of Labrador.

**Siddons** Oh I did, did I?

**Kemble** It had the excellent plan of civilising the Esquimaux Indians in order to employ them in the undertaking. Unfortunately the Esquimaux rose up, murdered everyone, turned the produce adrift on the ocean.

**Siddons** They obviously objected to being exploited by fools.

**Kemble** Anyway, he says you've lost everything.

**Siddons** He's consistent in his investments at least. My God that took me years, scrimping and saving. Slaving.

**Kemble** Well I've never liked him. He was the worst Gobbo I ever saw.

**Siddons** Rent one hundred guineas a year. Claret ninety-one. Twenty-nine pounds a year for the coachman. Coal twenty-six. Fifteen pounds per annum an efficient housekeeper. Eight pounds, scullery maid. Window tax one-and-six. We have thirteen windows. Eight shillings a yard of damask – fifteen for a frock. Seven shillings one pair stout shoes, George's feet grow phenomenally. Henry thank God has desisted in that department. French lessons for Cecilia, a pound for twelve. A month of dancing lessons for Sally, two pounds. Four shillings a pound of coffee. Sugar three pounds. Seven's a dozen rabbits. Three-and-six a fat chicken. Boot blacking is sixpence a block. We get through one of those a week. Threepence to the boy who sweeps the chimney. I spend tuppence a day on a bag of fruit. Pippins.

**Kemble** Your point is?

**Siddons** All I want is ten thousand pounds so I can retire to a cottage in the country.
I've toiled long enough for that!

**Kemble** That's not a cottage, that's a village.

**Siddons** A woman needs seven bedrooms. And wallpaper.

**Kemble** I'll try to head him off. For all the thanks I'll get. I'd be failing in my duty to Drury Lane if I took my eye off the box office.

**Siddons** Your devotion to that organ is biblical.

**Kemble** What's this?

**Siddons** My portrait money.

*He takes it. Puts it in his pocket.*

**Kemble** Your husband asked me to pick up anything of that sort for him. It shows I'm not taking sides.

*Exits.*

**Patti** He took the money.

**Siddons** Siddons maintains her queenly dignity.

*She gives an angry cry.*

You never heard that, Patti.

**Patti** No I didn't.

*A knock.*

I'll see them off shall I?

**Siddons** I couldn't possibly face another living being.

**Patti** She's not on the list. (*Reading a card that has been pushed under the door.*) 'The Honourable Lady Clara Morton-Abbey –'

**Siddons** Larpent's daughter. No ducking this one.

*Patti brings her in.*

**Clara** Siddons. I'm dazzled.

**Siddons** Don't be, I'm quite ordinary. Just Mrs William Siddons at home.

**Clara** But you're not at home. I waited till your visitors had left. Hid in the shadows. I don't know what came over me but watching you play tonight it's like someone else entered my body. So much feeling flooding through me. I've been here the past two nights. The same happened yesterday too.

**Siddons** Two consecutive nights! What dedication. I'll sign your programme.

**Clara** I watched your children being wrenched from you, at first I was so shocked I didn't feel anything, what I was seeing – it's the threat under everything – and then the woman next to me began to shake and she was making a wooing noise and her shaking began to make make me shake too and then I began to feel here – everything pressed down, the fear bubbling up in my chest and before I knew it there were great waves of pain like giving birth rushing through me and my mouth opened and I was woo-wooing too, in a kind of ecstasy. Waaah-waaaah we cried like great babies.

**Siddons**  The Siddons effect, never fails.

**Clara**  Which explains what's happened. Yesterday after the play I ran away.

**Patti**  How dramatic.

**Siddons**  Don't encourage her, Patti.

**Clara**  Hid in the park all night, came again today.

**Siddons**  My dear, you must go home – it's just a play.

**Clara**  They happen to us in a time and place like everything else.

**Patti**  That's true.

**Clara**  Tonight as I watched I felt the grief again but then something else.

**Siddons**  (*to Patti*) Show her the door, dear.

**Clara**  Coming out of me. I couldn't tell what but it was big.

**Siddons**  Patti will get you a carriage.

**Clara**  There's no point going home now. He told me if I ever ran away I'd never see the children again. That's the only bit of the play that rang untrue by the way. The ending.

**Siddons**  You have children?

**Clara**  Yes.

**Siddons**  You want to hold them again don't you?

**Clara**  Madly.

**Siddons**  My dear, your first duty is as a mother. I cannot be seen to be harbouring a deserter. Patti.

**Patti**  This way please.

**Clara** But what good does it do them to see their mother so unhappy and abused?

**Siddons** You must go home. Reason with him.

**Clara** He treats me unkindly. He says he will beat and pox his wife whenever he sees proper. Then the babies are born sick and they die.

**Patti** That's awful.

**Siddons** Don't think I don't sympathise. But my situation here is more fragile than it appears. Certain people long to embroil me in scandal. You are not to tell anyone what you've told us here. You must never say that this play or my part in it had anything to do with you abandoning your children.

Promise me.

**Clara** I promise.

**Siddons** And don't mention the feeling you had.

**Clara** I don't know what it was.

**Siddons** Good. Bury it.

**Clara** Where will I go?

**Siddons** Home, Clara, my dear, there's nowhere else to go.

*Pause.*

**Clara** Very well.

*She turns to go, then:*

It was rage. That was the feeling.

**Siddons** I never feel that. Goodbye. I'm thrilled you enjoyed my performance.

*Clara exits.*

Siddons changes her mind, runs after her to embrace her, draw her back in, save her.

*She doesn't.*

Last night I dreamt of Maria. She said, 'Have you got time to turn my sheet music?' She always had an uncanny knack of doing that just as I was leaving for the theatre.

Patti, you're such a help to me. Let me hold you. You won't mind, you're from Barnsley. I can't bear to be playing those parts, Mrs Halle and the rest.

**Patti** Because they miss their children so much?

**Siddons** No, because they're so perfect. It's killing me.


### FOUR

*Rehearsal.*

**Charles** Cowslip! Darling!
    They let you out did they? How's the family?

**Cowslip** My own girls will have nothing to do with me, poisoned against me by their father, Mr Topham, due to a short spell of incarceration I endured.

**Charles** Debtors' prison will be so much duller without you.

**Cowslip** It's marvellous to be working again.

**Charles** I last saw you in *The Winter's Tale*. You did a splendid bear.

**Charles** The costume was infested.

**Arthur** Bit like my digs.

**Charles** I spent a fortune on creams.

**Siddons** Rehearsals. A kind of chaos one must endure before a play is fit for the public.

**Cowslip** (*singing*) Jove loved an eagle
    Mars adored a lion

Venus kissed a pigeon
My lad's name is Brian.
Fusty rusty. Am I in luck?
Yes cos he's gonna give me
A right good –

**Siddons** Mary Wells, a comic actress.

**Cowslip** – roast duck.
That's from *The Agreeable Surprise*? 'The face and figure of Mrs Wells were admirably suited to the part of Cowslip the rosy-faced dairy maid imparting her with abundant excellence and exquisite –'

**Siddons** Why have you been employed?

**Cowslip** Ankles. This is my comeback.

**Siddons** Surely a mistake.

**Cowslip** The King will be glad to see me.

**Siddons** The last time he laid eyes on you you'd sailed alongside his boat dressed as Cleopatra, singing the national anthem sitting astride a cannon.

**Cowslip** He was charmed.

**Siddons** They pushed you away with oars.

**Cowslip** So very jealous of your royal patronage.

**Siddons** Which I achieved through excellence not a stunt.

**Cowslip** Is it because I have a bigger muff?

**Siddons** I have no interest in your muff.

**Cowslip** (*to another actor*) She goes about very elegant holding a little muff. So I got one that was bloody enormous.

**Siddons** Stand further off.

*Kemble enters.*

**Kemble** As you were.

**Siddons** You agreed I was to choose the next play.

**Kemble** That was just something I said. You can't tolerate the wounded mothers. I'm not unsympathetic. I've found a new tragedy.
(*Addresses the company.*) Thank you, company.
*De Monfort* is a terrifically edgy new work written by a mystery author.

**All** Oooh. Was it you, Arthur?

*Laughter.*

**Kemble** Much as we appreciate Arthur's talents as second juve lead I don't think he can be described as a literary giant.

**Arthur** I couldn't compose a flyer.

**Kemble** What is new in this writer I hear you ask?

**Siddons** Yes, we do ask.

**Kemble** Though noble in every way, De Monfort, the protagonist, whom I shall be playing –

**Siddons** Who shall I be playing?

**Kemble** His *loyal* sister Jane, perhaps you can pick up some tips. De Monfort is a man in the grip of a single deadly passion. Jealousy.

**Siddons** You should play that very well, brother.

**Charles** Oh beware my lord of jealousy!

**Arthur** It is the green-eyed monster which doth mock the meat it feeds on!

**Charles** Iago and Othello were both in love with Roderigo. Fireworks! Iago fell into the orchestra pit.

**Cowslip** Pushed.

**Kemble** Thank you. De Monfort can't bear the existence of his rival Rezenvelt, who once *spared his life* in a duel. Now he wants to destroy him. The very man he owes everything to. Genius, isn't it?

**Siddons** Where is the writer?

**Kemble** No one knows. That's why I called it a mystery. I've put a notice up outside the theatre asking him to declare himself. He'll be nervous clergy. They tend to approach the theatre with trepidation.

**Cowslip** As if we were frightening.

**Charles** Darling, you're terrifying. Especially when you don't like your costume.

**Kemble** May we continue? We're used to seeing my sister suffer onstage with me standing around looking at her but just imagine a man suffering to the same degree. How much more affecting that would be?

**All** Oh yes.

**Cowslip** I've forgotten how to cry – what's the point? No one takes any notice, not like when you do it onstage.

**Kemble** The extreme sensitivity of De Monfort marks him as a man of genius to which I humbly aspire to do justice.

**Actors** You will, Kemble. You're amazing. You'll blow the roof off. (*Etc.*)

**Kemble** He weeps profusely.

**Cowslip** I used to be able to cry out of either eye. Mr Garrick taught me.

**Kemble** In this character we have the feminine virtue of empathy mixed with the sublime masculine depth of being. Supercharged emotion. I'm longing to inflict it on the audience.

**Actors** Extraordinary, original. I can remember Garrick, you're his equal. (*Etc.*)

**Siddons** So if you're doing all the suffering what is there for me to do?

**Kemble** You'll find some business.
Thank you. Beginners!

**Charles** Darling, you can always upstage. Imagine you've discovered an absolutely fascinating beetle crawling on a downstage collar. Draws the eye.

**Siddons** Amateur.

**Kemble** Act One, Scene One. Jerome's house, a large old-fashioned chamber.

*They open their scripts.*

Enter Jerome bearing a light . . .

**Charles** Will this be a light from medieval times or now?

**Kemble** Leave that to props, Charles.

**Charles** Because I'm allergic to goose fat and it tends to dribble.

**Kemble** De Monfort is discovered in disconsolate pose. (*He writes in pencil.*) Possibly weeping? Enter Jane De Monfort, his sister.
Just to set the scene – she's come to comfort him. She is a woman while he is all raging passion and planet-sized emotion. Imagine a wren supplicating to a lion.

**Kemble** (*as De Monfort*)
I pray thee, sister, be contented.

*Siddons begins reading in a lacklustre manner, but as the scene progresses she begins to understand that Jane is an unusual woman character and warms to her task.*

35

**Siddons** (*as Jane*)
What, must I like a distant humble friend
Observe thy restless eye and gait disturbed
In timid silence? O no! De Monfort
Thy true trusted friend I will be.

**Kemble** (*as De Monfort*)
Ah, Jane, forbear!

**Siddons** (*as Jane*)
Then fy upon it! Fy upon it, De Monfort!

**Kemble** (*as De Monfort*)
Ask of me no more. Would I could tell thee!

**Siddons** (*as Jane*)
Then secret let it be
I'll stay by thee, I'll cheer thee, comfort thee
Pursue with thee the study of some art
Of nobler science that compels the mind
To steady thought till thou with brow unclouded
Smil'st again.

**Kemble** (*as De Monfort*)
It is hate, black, lasting, deadly hate
Which hath driven me forth from kindred peace.

**Siddons** (*as Jane*)
De Monfort, this is fiendlike, frightful, terrible
Strive with it, my brother
Strive bravely with it, drive it from thy breast
'Tis the degrader of a noble heart
Curse it and bid it part!
Come to my closet free from all intrusion
I'll school thee there and thou again shall be
My willing pupil and my generous friend
The noble Monfort, I have loved so long
And must not, will not lose.

*Kemble appears pacified. The company breaks into
applause. Kemble assumes it's for him but it's for Siddons.*

**Charles** I'm quite affected by her rhetorical prowess.

**Cowslip** She's ballsy.

**Charles** The wren ate the lion.

**Kemble** Yes, well done, sister, yes.

## FIVE

*The dressing room.*

**Siddons** Enter Siddons, statuesque, dark eyes, dark hair, she moves like a woman of superior rank.

*She throws something in the air joyfully or dances.*

Opening night of *De Monfort*.

*Joanna enters.*

**Patti** Laundry?

**Joanna** No.

**Patti** If you want an autograph you must wait at stage door with everyone else.

**Joanna** I'm the writer. Of *De Monfort*.

**Patti** Writer? That's a first – to get in to see you.

**Siddons** Well they're mostly dead so they don't usually knock.

**Joanna** Joanna Baillie.

**Siddons** I'm afraid I'm very busy, preparing internally.

**Joanna** I really did write it.

**Siddons** The theatre is a magnet for hangers-on who imagine they are artists. Some of them become critics, the rest must be encouraged to limit themselves to the purchasing of tickets.

**Joanna** When my publisher sent me the note saying my play was being considered at Drury Lane –

**Patti** You fainted?

**Joanna** No. I was ecstatic. I ran up and down the stairs fifteen times.

**Siddons** A real writer would be straight down the pub. Show her door, Patti.

**Joanna** My artistic goal is to get right inside the minds of my characters. To dig deep – find the stranger inside, let them face themselves truthfully for the first time.

**Siddons** Are you still here? Bleating on.

**Joanna** I think theatre is a school.

**Siddons** Don't start spreading that around, we'll never sell any tickets.

**Joanna** It can teach us about the passions and by reflecting on them furnish us with self-knowledge. That's how to change the world.

**Siddons** Ideals are commendable but nowadays one just wants to remember one's lines and not set the curtains on fire. Go home and when you wake up tomorrow this mania will have evaporated and you can busy yourself decorating a hat.

**Joanna** My brother is surgeon to the King. When I was ten I learnt to read. He taught me.

**Siddons** Perhaps your brother's natural modesty has stopped him from claiming authorship?

**Joanna** I wrote it. He wrote *The Morbid Anatomy of Some of the Most Important Parts of the Human Body*. He's taken a good look inside and so have I, in a different way. My interest in narrative began early. I had a thing for ghosts as a child.

**Patti** Ghosts?

**Joanna** Aye. They were the only stories I wanted to hear. It was my old nurse that told them to me – I'd go down to the servants of an evening, sit with them. Wouldn't be satisfied till I was absolutely petrified.

**Siddons** What a charming child you must have been.

**Joanna** I became addicted to clambering around the roof of the house to act out stories for the local kids. I learnt a lot from them. Then I saw you as Isabella in *The Fatal Marriage*. I acted it out to my family and the servants. They were laughing at first but they ended up crying. I thought, I like this power.

**Siddons** I'm not aware of the power, I'm afraid.

**Joanna** When I came to London I made sure to see you in everything. Went to the British Library, read every play I could lay my hands on. One day at home, seeing a quantity of white paper lying on the floor, it came into my head that I might write something on it and that something might be a play. I know women write comedy but I had the idea of writing about the stronger passions. I went darker.

**Siddons** Jane De Monfort is a mature woman. Past her grand climacteric.

**Joanna** Knocking fifty. Aye.

**Siddons** She never married?

**Joanna** No. She wasn't interested. She's a scholar.

**Siddons** She doesn't die. I usually do.

**Joanna** Gives excellent advice, which her brother ignores, takes over after his death, commands the respect of the whole town.

**Siddons** Well you've obviously read the play.

**Joanna** Think about it – what man has a notion of mentioning a woman after the age of five-and-twenty or of writing her as a rational being?

**Siddons** Yes.

**Patti** Does that mean –?

**Siddons** We are faced with the author of *De Monfort* after all.

**Patti** Congratulations.

**Joanna** Shall I inform Mr Kemble?

**Siddons** On no account. Your authorship is a disaster. You must let *De Monfort* be received upon its own merits. Everyone's been going on about how intelligent the writer is and if they know it's you they're going to feel really stupid.

*Kemble enters.*

**Kemble** I mean this stuff he says in the intro. That's new. 'Each man is ruled by a fatal passion which eats away at him like a deadly flesh-eating spider.' We could be looking at the greatest theatre mind of the decade.

**Joanna** Thank you.

**Patti** She's laundry.

**Siddons** Yes. Patti, show her the soils.

*Kemble catches sight of Patti.*

**Kemble** And who is this?

**Siddons** This is Patti Wilkinson. You employed her. She's been here a month.

**Kemble** Of course. Yes. Have you seen me perform, Patti?

**Patti** Every night.

**Kemble** And what is your considered opinion?

**Patti** I can always hear you.

**Kemble** Right. Well that is not an inconsiderable skill in this place. It's huge. Is Patti free? I need a button sewing on my waistcoat.

**Siddons** I don't share Patti. Try wardrobe.

*He exits.*

Joanna Baillie, welcome.

### SIX

*Onstage,* De Monfort.
*The actors/townspeople stand around Siddons/Jane De Monfort.*

**Actors** (*as townspeople*) Lady, we the townspeople await you.

**Siddons** (*as Jane*) First let us honour De Monfort who, unbalanced by hate, struck at his own life. Farewell, brother. I pledge to serve you, my people, faithfully, with heart and mind.

**Actors** (*as townspeople*) And we your grateful townspeople, will say we were never better served.

(*Singing.*) Awake our drowsy souls.
And burst the slothful band.
The wonders of this day.
Our noblest songs demand.

## SEVEN

*Siddons enters after the first performance of* De Monfort.
*Patti is waiting.*

**Siddons** It's extraordinary what not dying can do for you.
Siddons is absolutely ravenous.

*Patti brings the tray of food.*

Have you noticed something, Patti?

**Patti** You're not on the couch.

*Joanna enters.*

**Siddons** Well?

**Joanna** Do you ever have those dreams where you're in
a strange old house?
  You wander up a gloomy staircase and come upon
a great wooden door, you push it open and find a room you
never saw before, spacious and filled with light. It was there
the whole time and you never knew.

**Patti** That means she liked it.

**Siddons** Did I do her justice?

**Joanna** From the moment you entered – there was Jane –

**Siddons** She was, wasn't she?

**Joanna** Larger than life. Philosophising.

**Siddons** She interrupts men.

**Joanna** You were beyond my wildest expectations.
Thrilling!

**Siddons** Only the first night. Plenty of room to grow.

*Kemble enters with Boaden.*

**Kemble**  Why does everyone always come to your dressing room and not mine? Is it the cushions? That was one of my best. Certainly up there with my Coriolanus.

**Boaden**  Certainly up there.

**Kemble**  You just feel it sometimes. Everything hitting its mark. Boaden, your diagnosis? Perhaps when you've finished my sister's book you may now want to begin mine?

**Boaden**  Siddons.

**Kemble**  I did a lot of crying. Quite exhausting.

**Boaden**  I must have seen you perform a thousand times but tonight you showed me something different.

**Kemble**  Actual tears.

**Boaden**  A kind of –

**Siddons**  Command?

**Boaden**  Yes. That's it.

*He writes.*

**Siddons**  An intellectual and moral depth.

**Boaden**  Perhaps.

**Kemble**  I wouldn't go that far.

**Siddons**  She discovers her capacity for ethical leadership.

**Boaden**  Certainly.

**Siddons**  Yes, write that.

**Kemble**  Right. I weep a lot in my part. At one point I fall off my chair.

**Boaden**  Whatever it was you showed me, Siddons, it was sublime in a new way.

**Kemble**  Heightened sensitivity in a man is a sign of genius.

**Joanna**  The cleverest character is Jane by far.

**Kemble**  The play is called *De Monfort*.

**Joanna**  That's her name too.

**Kemble**  Stick to laundry.

**Boaden**  I don't think we can ascribe an intention to the author, he isn't here.

**Siddons**  Beyond thrilled you enjoyed me.

*Boaden starts to exit.*

**Kemble**  Boaden, let's talk reviews.

*Kemble follows him off.*

**Joanna**  I'm the writer of *De Monfort*. It's a success but nobody knows. I'm like a kind of ghost.

**Siddons**  You're my writer. Flesh and blood. Have a little patience. I've played Mrs Halle for one hundred and forty-seven performances. I can't stand the woman.

**Joanna**  If they find out who I really am they'll hate me because I lied.

**Siddons**  Tell her, Patti.

**Patti**  It stays in this room.
   The blue stockings came tonight. They sent a note. I told them we couldn't fit sixteen into the dressing room. They're waiting in the foyer. They want you to do them the honour of letting them tell you how tremendous they think you are.

**Siddons**  I can spare a few minutes for that.

*Siddons exits.*

**Patti**  She's actually happy. You've done that.

**Joanna** I don't think I've ever made anyone happy before.

*Kemble re-enters.*

**Kemble** Boaden's had to rush off. So, Patti, you got to see my De Monfort? And?

**Patti** Yes. Why did he keep saying 'orner'?

**Kemble** No that's 'honour'.

**Patti** Oh. I'll just need to –

*She has to manoeuvre to avoid Kemble, who stands too close.*
  *Joanna is left alone with him.*

**Joanna** Siddons is off to see her fans.

**Kemble** Her loyal succubi.

**Joanna** Did Mr Boaden like it?

**Kemble** 'It's your sister's triumph, old fellow.' You see, I've seen her do all that before. I know her tricks.

**Joanna** You were splendid too. Particularly the way you handled the anagnorisis in Act Three.

*Pause.*

**Kemble** So how is laundry?

**Joanna** Okay. You know.

**Kemble** What's the toughest stain to get out?

**Joanna** I'm not laundry.

**Kemble** No. It's candle grease. Are you the one who's been stealing from the dressing rooms?

**Joanna** I wrote *De Monfort*.

**Kemble** No you didn't. You're a woman. Don't be ridiculous. Oh.

**Joanna** Yes. I know it's terrible news. I don't like lying but I don't want to prejudice the town against my play.

**Kemble** What you were saying about Jane being cleverer. Say more about that.

**Joanna** It's not what I intended when I started to write. It was all about him.

**Kemble** Yeah.

**Joanna** But this really weird thing happened where I found her more interesting. I kind of had to hold her back from taking over the play.

**Kemble** Shit.

**Joanna** I mean when you think about it – he's hampered by an outmoded and useless masculine pride that he wears like a great big ugly excrescence. She is just way more impressive. She's had to overcome barriers. She did that on her own. Just through thinking about it and reading books.

**Kemble** Swotty type.

*Pause.*

I think it's time.

**Joanna** Time?

**Kemble** To let the town know who you are. To claim your own property. Enough with the speculation.

**Joanna** To put my own name to my own play?

**Kemble** A notice in the morning papers would do it. Honesty is the best policy.

**Joanna** Drury Lane Theatre. I can't believe it. Me.

## EIGHT

**Siddons** Second-night syndrome, a tendency to be complacent after the success of the first, which can result in mumbling, stumbling and failures to enter.

*Onstage*, De Monfort.
    *Officers appear.*

(*As Jane.*) Where is my brother, the noble De Monfort?

**Officer 2** That's just what we were saying.

**Officer 1** What's happened to the prisoner I asked you to keep an eye on?

**Officer 2** He appears to be not present, sir.

**Officer 1** Hark, I think I hear his approach.

*Pause.*

No, my mistake.

**Officer 2** So what's everyone been up to?

*Kemble enters.*

**Officer 1** He's here. Thank God.

**Siddons** At last, noble brother.

*Kemble begins to die. This is noisy and unpleasant. He drags this dying out.*

Have you no last words for me?

*He dies.*

Brother? No last words?

**Officer 1** He's passed.

**Kemble** Death's stroke has come.

*He dies again.*

**Officer 1** *and* **Officer 2** Now he's passed.

**Siddons** And without a farewell speech exhorting me to bend to no one a suppliant knee. Alas he died a little earlier than anticipated. Farewell, noble De Monfort.

*She exits.*

NINE

*Patti is alone, preparing the dressing room for the end of the second performance of* De Monfort.
*Kemble enters in costume, with a bloody red blooming cloth at his breast, the 'self-inflicted' wound of De Monfort.*

**Kemble** (*indicates his wound*) I died early. Ten minutes before the curtain while she instructs the townspeople. The play is over once I'm dead. But no – the writer is rattling on.

**Patti** I like it.

**Kemble** Do you? You're qualified are you? To give an opinion.

**Patti** I just know what I like.

**Kemble** Don't deny me, Patti.

**Patti** Deny you what?

**Kemble** I want you. Here, now. In my sister's dressing room.

**Patti** I have her supper to lay out.

**Kemble** Don't play coy.
You're a good-looking girl, Patti, don't pretend this doesn't happen all the time.

**Patti** What doesn't?

**Kemble** I'm obsessed. You're on my mind day and night, constantly. You witch. What are you doing?

48

**Patti** Just a bit of tidying.

**Kemble** Doing to me I meant.

*He grabs her.*

Ripe little apricot.

*She instinctively grabs hold of his hair, this hurts him, they struggle. He breaks free.*

I'm the manager of this theatre!

*Kemble is defeated.*

You've made me late for my bow.

*He exits.*
*Patti is shaken. She puts on a protective layer of clothing immediately.*
*Offstage, sound of sporadic applause.*
*Siddons and Kemble enter.*

**Siddons** You threw the play!

**Kemble** I won't have that, sister.

**Siddons** Stepping on my lines. Pauses big enough to drive a hearse through. Coughing. Fluffing. Excessively loud dying.
  Then that weird twisty thing you do with your mouth when your concentration is zapped.

**Kemble** Face it. The technical term for this play is 'a turkey'.

**Siddons** You loved it when you thought it was by a vicar!

*Joanna enters with Boaden.*

**Kemble** What's everyone saying, Boaden?

**Boaden** Sir Walter Scott is saying it's hard to believe that this rather commonplace individual could have conceived the potent deadly hatred of De Monfort.

**Siddons** How can she be commonplace?

**Joanna** I'm a female playwright.

**Boaden** The first-night buzz was good. People were intrigued, but this morning after her declaration they started thinking how likely was it that such an exalted being as De Monfort would be ruled by one single passion? Jealousy? A man's mind is a highly evolved organism.

**Patti** They can be obsessed.

**Boaden** For a woman that may be true, they are more easily subdued by emotion, but for a man not so much and this is the town's gripe.

**Joanna** It's ridiculous that in this day and age a woman can't own up to writing a play without it prejudicing its reception.

**Siddons** What possessed you to think that honesty was the best policy?

**Kemble** Who would have known?

**Siddons** So it was your idea! Iago!

**Kemble** Tepid applause tonight.

**Siddons** Tomorrow will be better.

**Boaden** Advance bookings?

**Kemble** Dismal.

**Siddons** Give them a chance to warm to it, brother.

**Boaden** What are you going to do?

**Kemble** Withdraw the play.

**Siddons** Too hasty.

**Boaden** Cut your losses.

**Joanna** Can he do that?

**Kemble** It's my theatre.

**Siddons** If you do that I won't step foot on that stage again. For a season. Feel that in your box office.

**Boaden** Sibling strife? Perhaps a touch of Lady Macbeth after all?

*Siddons and Kemble repeat their* Macbeth *routine.*

**Siddons** No, no. We never argue.

**Kemble** It's dead in the water.

**Joanna** I had friends coming tomorrow tonight. What do I tell them?

**Boaden** I suppose you'll go back to what you were doing before.

**Joanna** I had nothing to do before.

**Siddons** This was your first go. Did Shakespeare let *Titus Andronicus* put him off? An experimental tragedy about a pie. You've just begun. I swallowed Jane De Monfort in one great gulp, like a thirsty traveller. I want to keep drinking.

**Boaden** She's so fabulous.

**Joanna** I'm reeling.

**Siddons** Finding you, it's like Ulysses sighting Ithaca after ten years at sea.

**Boaden** Oh wonderful.

**Siddons** Like a visitor arriving in dismal darkness, awakening next morning, flinging open the window and seeing a sparkling view of rolling verdant hills.

**Boaden** I'm there.

**Siddons** Like shovelling dung and turning up gold.

**Boaden** Wow.

**Joanna** I failed.

**Siddons** Write me another play. Now I've been Jane I can't go back to the milksops.

**Kemble** You see – you despise playing distressed mothers!

**Siddons** That's slander, Mr Boaden.
(*To Joanna.*) I'll always receive you. Don't forget. Promise me.

*Joanna exits.*
*Boaden gets out his notebook, starts taking notes.*

**Kemble** You're touring Ireland.

**Siddons** No.

**Kemble** Didn't your husband tell you? You're leaving tomorrow. You're doing *Hamlet*. Dublin. Smock Alley.

**Siddons** Any actor with any ambition is trying to leave Smock Alley. There are no boxes. No one listens. They're too busy arguing with each other and slurping oysters.

**Kemble** Returning via the north. Edinburgh. Liverpool. Leeds. York. Birmingham. Hull. Back for the summer season at Drury Lane. He's signed the contracts.

**Siddons** I could tear them up.

**Kemble** You'd be sued.

**Boaden** A sniff of conflict?

**Siddons** Oh no no. No.

**Boaden** The masculine overcoming your feminine aspect?

**Siddons** That's not in my nature. I worry about Sally.

**Kemble** Apparently she'll be fine, you fret too much. See you in four months.

**Siddons**  Yes, brother dear.

**Boaden**  How charming you will be visiting your immeasurable talents upon the provinces and over the sea. I'll make a start on the memoirs.

**Kemble**  About the memoirs.

*They exit.*

**Siddons**  Siddons graciously takes leave of her surroundings. She relishes the opportunity to share her gifts far and wide. Wonderful. Wonderful.

*She picks up an item of clothing and rips it in half with a roar.*
  *Siddons hands it to Patti.*

Can you mend that?

**Patti**  I can try.

**Siddons**  You never saw me do that, Patti. She isn't me. Interval.

*Nothing happens.*

Interval!

*It happens.*

# Part Two

## ONE

*Siddons about to start fencing with Galindo, a Spanish fencing teacher. She responds with each move.*

**Siddons** Dublin. A city of poets, Guinness, and Guinness in poets. Siddons in training. The woman does nothing by halves. The audience must never see the work that goes on behind the scenes. For the truth of the character she would sacrifice everything. But Hamlet in breeches? Legs are only appropriate in comedy. I'm doing him in a dress.

**Galindo** En garde!

**Siddons** Siddons is too grand for legs.

**Galindo** Passe avant.

**Siddons** My brother plays Hamlet in London, I'm allowed Dublin.

**Galindo** Parry.

**Siddons** He can't take the competition. Did I say that aloud? How marvellous. Dear Galindo, why did I leave it so long, learning to fence? I adore it. Have you found this before?

**Galindo** I never teach lady before. Riposte.

**Siddons** It's very dangerous. You musn't ever do it again.

**Galindo** Balestra. You no like?

**Siddons** Yes I do like and that's the trouble. I wake up in the morning and I count the hours till my next lesson.

**Galindo** My wife say 'Why Siddons need so many?'

**Siddons** Because I have to kill three men.

**Galindo** On stage only.

**Siddons** Sadly the tips are blunted.

**Galindo** My wife is very jealous woman.
  She say if she ever find that we – she put letter in all London newspaper.

**Siddons** Tell her she only has to do a couple, the rest will pick it up. You have to make her feel loved.

**Galindo** That is problem. Because lately in the marriage bed . . .

**Siddons** You have to try harder – pretend – it can't be that difficult if women can do it. I hardly ever see my husband. He's bunked up with his mistress in Kingston. Gets me off the hook! It's wonderful the things you can say when you're out of the country.

**Galindo** I want open school.

**Siddons** Everyone deserves to learn to wield a sword as deftly as you do.

**Galindo** In London.

**Siddons** A pound a lesson or three for four. Charge for the loan of a rapier.

**Galindo** I have no capital.

**Siddons** I could do a benefit for you.
  Give you the money before my husband got hold of it.
  My return, twenty-five per cent till the debt was paid then fifteen in perpetuity.

**Galindo** Ten?

**Siddons** Twelve.
  This is such a deep conversation.

  *At this critical moment an actor enters.*

55

**Scraggs** Am I interrupting?

**Siddons** We're rehearsing.

**Scraggs** Percy Scraggs, actor.

I was supposed to be playing Rozencrantz and Player Queen but I broke three of my phalanges when some joker put the throne on my foot. So that was that. Anyway, I was wondering if you've had any further thoughts about doing a benefit on my behalf, donating the proceeds of the performance to me because it would really help me out. I have a family to feed. Me the missus and little Percy and that boy's sprouting like a celery. I sent you a letter yesterday and had expected a reply by now but the humble must wait on the great, 'twas ever thus.

**Siddons** Siddons is politeness itself. Get out, you nobody!!

*She runs at him with a sword.*
*He exits.*
*Patti enters. She is holding a letter.*

**Patti** From England. It says urgent. It's about Sally.

**Siddons** Read it to me.

*Patti doesn't.*

Go now, dear Galindo.

*Galindo exits.*

Siddons has a sixth sense.
Siddons knows the news is bad.

*Siddons drops to her knees.*

Is she . . .?

## TWO

*Dressing room. Siddons on the couch, a single candle.*
*Enter Kemble.*

**Kemble** Sarah? We've partnered each other for twenty
years. I know you made your name first but I've never held
that against you. Much. We need you back at work. Say by
Tuesday.

**Siddons** Two daughters dead.

**Kemble** Yes. We've had a bit of a disaster here while you've
been away. *Vortigern* played at a massive loss. Turns out it
wasn't by Shakespeare after all. Some Irish lad taking the
piss. We bled at the box office. We need something reliable.
*The Distressed Mother* alternating with *The Stranger.*
Camelot cost a fortune to build. The fucking moat. Swans
plus swan handler. He's cornered the market. Charges by
the feather.

**Siddons** Brother. I am losing my way.

**Kemble** You're on the couch.

**Siddons** I'm slowly freezing over.

**Kemble** What, like freezing?

**Siddons** You know when we enter into a part and it calls
on us to bring forth a particular emotion and we search our
memory for a time when we experienced such a feeling for
ourselves?

*Pause.*

**Kemble** Yes.

**Siddons** Which is a kind of joy because when our feelings
are fresh to us they hit the audience most unexpectedly and
delightfully.

**Kemble** Right.

**Siddons**  Well that . . . is compromised.

**Kemble**  Wait, you're saying that is acting?

**Siddons**  Yes.

**Kemble**  And you're telling me this now?

**Siddons**  I don't follow you, brother.

**Kemble**  You've kept this secret from me all this time and never thought to share it?

**Siddons**  I imagined you felt the same too.

**Kemble**  Well, no, I didn't. In all our twenty years it never occurred to you to mention it?
     Unbelievable. Kept it to yourself for your own advantage.

**Siddons**  I can tell you now, brother, it's not too late.

**Kemble**  No thank you, I don't want your charity.

**Siddons**  It comes from here.

*She places her hand on his solar plexus.*

You have to breathe into here.
     You have been accused of a certain woodenness –

**Kemble**  Damn their eyes, 'woodenness'.

**Siddons**  Breathe.

*Kemble takes a shallow breath.*

Deeper.

*Kemble does. He begins to visibly relax.*

Now connect it with an emotion and aspirate on a sound.

**Kemble**  Ha!

**Siddons**  What was that?

**Kemble**  Contempt.

**Siddons**  That's an attitude. Try fear.

**Kemble**  Fear?

**Siddons**  Yes.

**Kemble**  HA!

**Siddons**  That was just louder. Remember when we were children and we waited in the dark for the carts. And we waited and we waited.

**Kemble**  Yes.

**Siddons**  And it began to dawn on us that in all the bustle we had been forgotten. We couldn't believe it, surely Ma and Pa would appear and embrace us, take us with them, but there we sat in the rain abandoned in the dark and that stranger approached us, we told him our parents had left us by mistake but he laughed and said we were left forever because we were bad, ungrateful children, he grabbed us, dragged us into the woods, said he would slit our throats if we made a sound and he took our clothes. He said stay there or I'll come find you, bleed you out like pigs, remember? We waited in the woods all night, holding each other trembling in anguish at each rustle of leaves believing he had returned. Now try.

*Kemble gives a true howl of fear. It shakes him.*

Better.

**Kemble**  No. My diphthongs were all over the place. It's nonsense. There's nothing you can tell me about acting. I'm John Philip Kemble.

**Siddons**  I need a writer. Joanna Baillie.

**Kemble**  No one liked her play.

**Siddons**  They liked it well enough till you turned them against it.
    The thing is, brother, I'm not twenty-five any more.

**Kemble** No you're not.

**Siddons** I've grown but my parts have not.

**Kemble** I haven't got the faintest idea what you're talking about.

**Siddons** What's inside me needs to be channelled into the roles I play.

**Kemble** This isn't going to get anatomical is it?

*Siddons throws herself back on the couch.*

**Siddons** Give me what I want, brother, or fear the consequences.

*She blows out the candle.*
*He goes to leave as Patti enters.*

**Kemble** Patti. Looking very – well I don't know – padded. It suits you.

*He exits.*
*Patti relights the candle.*

**Patti** Can't have you here in the dark.
It's Joanna.

*Siddons gets up. Sits at her desk.*
*Joanna enters.*

**Siddons** (*reads from a letter*) 'Avaricious witch, in Ireland earning money while your daughter was –'

**Patti** Wickedness.

**Siddons** '– crying out for you with her last breath.'

**Joanna** You wanted to see me?

**Patti** Siddons has fallen into a lowness. These letters –

**Siddons** (*reads*) 'Your daughter's dead which you diserve.' 'Diserve' with an 'i'. That hurts. Sally was such a marvellous speller. When we got the letter saying Sally was ill we waited three days for the sea to calm before we could cross. We arrived too late.

**Joanna** I'm so sorry to hear that. If there's anything I can do –

**Patti** Write her a play. That would lift her spirits.

**Joanna** You can't just order a play like a new hat, a loaf of bread, a puppy.

**Siddons** I imagine you've already started haven't you? Scribbling away then hiding the pages? Little scenarios nibbling away at your brain. It's what you do. You can't run away from it.

**Joanna** I'm not writing a play to have it dropped after two performances.

**Siddons** I don't think you understand. I, Siddons, am asking you.

**Joanna** I'm sorry, I can't.

**Siddons** All I want is the female version of *Hamlet*. One thousand, four hundred and twenty-two lines. Madness, wit, grief, rage, love, fencing. The complete package.

**Joanna** I won't take up any more of your time.

**Siddons** There's no one else can do it. Destiny has alighted on you.
     Have you ever worn a dress that didn't fit? Too tight under the arms? The hem let down countless times but still it only just covers your knees? I've outgrown my parts. Something is growing in me. If I could cut it out of me I would but I can't. I'm not being greedy or selfish. It'll save my sanity and please my audience.

**Joanna** I don't know how I ever had the audacity to write in the first place. I was punished for it. I'm sorry.

**Siddons**  So that's a no?

**Joanna**  Yes. Regretfully.

**Siddons**  Very well. Siddons pauses, a moment of indecision, the calm before the storm.
Patti, pack away my costumes.

**Patti**  Oh no. I can't believe it.

**Siddons**  Throw my parts on the fire.

**Patti**  Okay.

**Siddons**  There's nothing here for me. I must lead a life of quiet contemplation out of the public eye growing my own vegetables.

**Joanna**  I know what you're doing? This is an act. To get me to write again.

**Siddons**  Siddons stopped. Siddons over. Finished. Kaput.
'For now they kill me with a living death.'

**Patti**  I expect I'll have to go back to marry Dicky Suet.

**Siddons**  It's too horrible to contemplate.

**Joanna**  I've had enough public humiliation for one lifetime thank you.

**Siddons**  If you lack the courage to face public humiliation you aren't an artist.

**Joanna**  Fine.

**Siddons**  I had my disappointments. Portia. Age nineteen. Chosen by Garrick to play here at Drury Lane. Pregnant. They dressed me in salmon. I wandered around the vast stage the colour of a boiled prawn and about as effective. My voice vanished in my throat. A huge misfire. My notices ranged from the unremarkable to the execrable. I left in disgrace. My first scar. The point is I came back. Five years later I came back and slayed them.

**Patti** I think if she doesn't get her way she will explode.

*Pause.*

**Joanna** Two nights ago I couldn't sleep – got out of bed, went to my desk.
I tried telling myself to stop but no.

*She searches around in her pockets pulls out some papers.*

I started writing something.

**Siddons** A play?

**Joanna** Yes, I suppose I have written a bit of a play.

**Patti** What's it about?

**Joanna** It's about this woman called Orra.

**Siddons** As in 'horror'?

**Joanna** As in 'aura'. Like gold. She's been imprisoned in a castle by one Hugobert, your basic bastard, unless she submits and marries his pointless son Glottenbal so they can get her lands. The priest asks her to pretend like a 'proper' woman but she despises flattery and subterfuge as the weapons of the weak. She refuses to put 'a nail in the coffin of my life'.

**Siddons** 'A nail in the coffin of my life.' Nice.

**Joanna** (*reads*) 'Must I be consigned with all my lands and rights into the hands of some proud man and say, "Take all, I pray, and do me in return the grace and favour to be my master"?'

**Siddons** Who hasn't had that thought?

**Patti** Does she escape?

**Joanna** There's a decent man, Theobald.

**Patti** Do I detect a hero and in the nick of time?

**Joanna** But he gets eaten by a bear.

**Patti** Oh dear.

**Siddons** Good. Increase her obstacles.

**Joanna** Orra is trapped. Locked away, threatened with rape by the rake Rudigere who preys on her captivity, waiting helplessly to be married to a man she despises –

**Patti** What does she do?

**Joanna** That's as far as I've got.

**Siddons** If she was Jane De Monfort she'd be rational about it. But then Jane had independent property due to a freak clause in her father's will and a knack of repelling men.

**Patti** There must be a way out for her?

**Joanna** I alway ask myself what the Greeks would have done?

**Patti** Built a wooden horse?

**Joanna** At extreme moments their protagonists are filled with the ecstasy of a God, transformed, like Cassandra. She receives the gift of prophecy but is cursed never to be believed.

**Siddons** Story of my life.

**Patti** Drives you mad when no one knows what you know or wouldn't believe you if you said it.

**Siddons** Drives you mad!

**Joanna** So – so – Orra takes the only alternative – she goes mad but not conveniently or quietly with herbs, she goes mad defiantly and with frightening eloquence swallows up the whole of the stage. She has the last word – thrusts a skull into the faces of her oppressors for all their petty power, they're only dirt in the end. She deconstructs the patriarchy.

**Siddons**  Write it. What do think, Patti?

**Patti**  Sounds like a good night out.

**Siddons**  Finish it.

**Joanna**  Of course. I'm just like any other writer. Desperate to get my play on.

*She exits.*

**Siddons**  Patti. You look bigger.

**Patti**  I'm wearing all my clothes at once.

**Siddons**  That's a thing is it?


### THREE

**Siddons**  Dramatic licence is efficacious for cutting waiting time.
   Writers are notoriously tardy.

*Joanna delivers a play to Siddons.*

**Joanna**  Here's the play.

**Siddons**  Thank you.

*Joanna exits.*
   *Kemble enters.*

**Kemble**  Writers, hard to shake.

**Patti**  Let me check the list.

**Kemble**  Really? When I know you're just longing to write my name on that piece of paper.
   This play *Orra*. It's a no.

**Siddons**  Patti. Get over to Covent Garden, tell Mr Harris I've finally given in to his desperate entreaties to offer my services at his theatre.

**Kemble**  You'd sink that low?

**Siddons**  When I play Drury Lane the house is invariably full, with tickets at six shillings, three-and-six and two shillings, three thousand six hundred seats the takings per night are –

**Patti**  One thousand four hundred and ten pounds four shillings.

**Siddons**  Without me halve that.

**Patti**  Seven hundred and five pounds and two shillings.

**Kemble**  What's my part?

**Siddons**  There's Theobald, the love interest.

**Kemble**  How many lines?

**Patti**  One hundred and thirteen.

**Kemble**  And you get?

**Patti**  Nine hundred and nine.

**Kemble**  Barely an eighth of yours.

**Siddons**  Welcome to my world.

**Kemble**  What happens to him?

**Patti**  He gets eaten by a bear.

**Kemble**  Fuck off.

**Siddons**  You could play Rudigere, the rake?

**Kemble**  That's not me.

**Siddons**  May I remind you of the Fanny De Camp affair.

**Kemble**  I apologised to her father. She was very pretty and she was standing around in the dark.

**Siddons**  Waiting in the wings to go on. She's an actress. What else was she supposed to do?

**Kemble** Have it your way. Take the reins for a show, how hard can it be if Kemble can do it? It's just Drury Lane Theatre. A gladiatorial pit! Hamartia, the fatal flaw, through which a character is brought low. And when the fall happens you will no doubt turn to me to scrape you off the floor.

(*To Patti.*) I'm Philip with one 'l'.

*He exits.*

**Siddons** Siddons looks for the truth of a character. If it's to be found in nature she knows it can be played. She goes in search of an angry madwoman. That shouldn't be too hard to find.


FOUR

*The madhouse.*

**Siddons** (*calling*) Turnkey?

*We hear the sounds of keys in a rusty lock.*
*Distant shrieks, cries, eerie singing.*
*Turnkey leads in Siddons.*

I was never here.

**Turnkey** I'm discreet. There's one I'll show ya.

*She takes out a baton, exits.*
*Turnkey comes back with an unwilling woman, Clara, whom we have met before. She is the worse for having been incarcerated for months.*

This lady has kindly come to visit you, she has an interest in madwomen.

**Clara** I'm not mad.

**Turnkey** Take care, the mad are cunning.

**Clara** My husband has a mistress.

**Turnkey** Babbles on like this.

**Clara** He spends my fortune. They won't let me see my children. Georgie is six, Mariah is five, Jane is four and Leonard is three-and-a-half.

**Turnkey** Mind your manners, Clara.

**Siddons** Clara. Oh my dear.

**Clara** Siddons! I went home. He locked me in the scullery, wouldn't let me see the children, put me in here. At night blood comes through the walls.

**Turnkey** She's always on about that. She smeared shit on the walls Friday.

**Clara** I apologised for it. I was angry. I can't explain it. It was a bad thing to do.

**Turnkey** Made her clean it up. With her own clothes.

**Siddons** Why?

**Turnkey** Teach her a lesson, she won't be doing it again.

**Clara** Why are you here?

**Turnkey** Not your place to ask!

**Siddons** I'm researching a play, *Orra*. She's forced to marry a man she loathes. Prefers to go mad.

**Clara** It's not very nice being mad.
  Because you don't think you are but everyone else does. And they dunk you in an ice bath. Help me.

*She grabs Siddons.*

**Turnkey** Back off!

**Clara** Tell my mother to come and get me or take me with you.

**Siddons** I can't do that. It's not in my power.

**Clara** Don't leave me! Being here, it's enough to drive you bloody mad.

*The Turnkey uses the baton as a threat.*

**Turnkey** Shame on you. Uttering a profanity.

**Clara** Help me!

**Siddons** Best thing is to keep it all inside, Clara. Pretend. Act.

**Turnkey** Get away now. You've had your chance at company. Go on back to your cell.

**Siddons** Siddons risks muckraking and scandal and carries Clara with her back to the world.


### FIVE

*Rehearsals.*

**Kemble** Well I'm here. Rehearsals. How's Vince?

**Charles** He's okay. He's shed all his tail hair. It's a mystery.

**Kemble** Ah. He was a wonderful Crab.

**Charles** Best part in Shakespeare. No lines, all the laughs.

**Kemble** Dog's life.

**Charles** Siddons in charge, eh, boss?

**Kemble** My sister's at a difficult age for a woman.
   I'm indulging her, giving her her head with this play. If you want to break in a horse, you tire it out first.

*Siddons enters, followed by Cowslip.*

**Cowslip** I was made to be on a stage. When I was a girl how I annoyed everyone!

**Siddons** Hardly a recommendation.

**Arthur**  Have you read the play?

**Charles**  Only my part.

**Cowslip**  With my singing 'Tiny foolish fluttering thing'.

**Charles**  I'm not paid enough to read the whole play.

**Cowslip**  I have a remarkable playing range, six to sixty. I can sing, I can dance, I can fit my whole body through a hoop. I'm prepared to start at three pounds a week.

**Siddons**  I wouldn't have you gratis.

**Cowslip**  Two?

**Siddons**  The stage is a dangerous place for a woman. It requires restraint to maintain one's virtue, which you do not possess. You're a strumpet.

**Cowslip**  I've only had three husbands.

**Siddons**  Simultaneously.

**Kemble**  Sister, audiences need some light relief.

**Siddons**  She's a comic turn. There's no job for you here with me.

**Cowslip**  You haven't got a heart in there, some sort of pump.

*She exits.*

**Arthur**  What do you think?

**Charles**  The best way to survive in this business is to adore everything you're in.

**Arthur**  How can you adore it if you haven't read it?

**Charles**  I'm acting I love it. It really works.

**Siddons**  Company. We have a guest.

**Actors**  A guest?

**Kemble** The rehearsal room is a sacred space, our temple. We do not admit philistines.

**Siddons** Mrs Larpent.

*She exits.*
  *Actors gasp.*

**Kemble** Or harpies.

*Enter Mrs Larpent.*

Mrs Larpent.

**Siddons** Anna, we don't want you to have another sudden change of heart mid-run.

**Mrs Larpent** No, that would be very inconvenient for the theatre.

**Kemble** Just a little bit.

**Siddons** We want to embrace you in our process.

**Mrs Larpent** I am a reasonable woman of a very malleable nature. I allowed *The Grecian Daughter* to go ahead – provided Euphrasia took out her breast and suckled her starving father *offstage*. It's not something one would wish to witness live, with sound effects. This play *Orra*. I've read it. The one redeeming male character gets eaten. So what's that saying?

**Siddons** Playing Orra extends my repertoire in an interesting new direction.

**Mrs Larpent** She's insane.

**Siddons** She's transformed through adversity into ecstatic prophetic utterance.

**Mrs Larpent** That's clever.

**Siddons** Theatre must reveal to us the truth so that we mend the world for our children.

**Mrs Larpent** You've left it very late to apply for the licence.

**Kemble** Very late.

**Siddons** Because I trust you to make the right decision, Anna. Welcome.

**Mrs Larpent** So this is a rehearsal. I've often wondered what goes on.

**Kemble** It's quite simple. Before we present a play to the audience we practise it first.

**Charles** We all sit around reading the play. We have tea. We put it on its feet. We have more tea. Sometimes we make a discovery.

**Mrs Larpent** Oh yes?

**Charles** For example if a scene isn't working, just play it as if your character is secretly in love. So for example 'This key's a bit stiff, I've been fiddling with it for hours' becomes 'This key's a bit stiff, I've been fiddling with it for hours'.

**Mrs Larpent** Oh yes that works. Well that's marvellous. And you find that one day of rehearsal adequate?

**Actors** Oh yes.

**Mrs Larpent** I'll be as quiet as a mouse.

**Siddons** Arthur – read the stage directions and keep it simple. No acting.

*Arthur nods.*

I shall be reading Orra. Kemble, Rudigere.
Patti is reading in for Catrina.

**Kemble** Where's our Catrina?

**Arthur** Giving birth. She's promised to be back in time for her half-hour call.

*Patti comes forward reluctantly. Picks up a script.*

72

**Arthur** (*overacting, reads*) A gothic room in a castle with the stage darkened. Enter Catrina bearing a light. Enter Rudigere, beckoning Catrina to him, and speaks to her in a low voice.

**Kemble** (*as Rudigere*) Go and prepare thy lady's chamber. Why dost thou ever closely near her keep?

**Patti** (*as Catrina*) She charged me so to do.

**Kemble** (*as Rudigere*) I charge thee also, with paramount authority to leave her. I for a while will take thy station here. Thou art not mad? Thou dost not hesitate?

**Arthur** (*reading stage directions*) Fixing his eyes on her with a fierce threatening look from which she shrinks. Exit Catrina. Enter Orra.

*Patti exits scene.*

**Siddons** (*as Orra*) This was the home of lawless, bloody power. The very air rests thick and heavily where murder hath been done. There is a strange oppression in my breast. Catrina, does thou not feel a close unwholesome vapour?

**Kemble** (*as Rudigere*) No, ev'ry air to me is light and healthful that with thy sweet and heavenly breath is mixed.

**Siddons** (*as Orra*) You here!

**Arthur** (*reading stage directions*) Looking around.

**Siddons** (*as Orra*) And Catrina gone?

*Patti is reacting to this offstage, it's too close for comfort.*

**Kemble** (*as Rudigere*) Does Orra fear to be alone with one whose being on her favour hangs?

**Siddons** (*as Orra*) I choose to be alone.

**Kemble** (*as Rudigere*) You choose it here in such a place, so near the midnight hour. How loathed and irksome must my presence be.

**Siddons** (*as Orra*) Do you deride my weakness?

**Kemble** (*as Rudigere*) I deride it? No, noble maid, say rather than from you I have a kindred weakness caught. I feel by sympathy.

**Siddons** (*as Orra*) Do you too such human weakness own?

**Kemble** (*as Rudigere*) We are all creatures in the wakeful hour of ghastly midnight, formed to cower together forgetting all distinctions of the day.

**Arthur** (*reading stage directions*) Stealing closer to her as he speaks and putting his arms around her. Orra breaking from him.

**Siddons** (*as Orra*) I pray thee hold thy parley further off. Why do you press so near me?

**Kemble** (*as Rudigere*) And are thou so offended, lovely Orra?

**Siddons** (*as Orra*) Off, fiend! Let snakes and vipers cling to me so thou dost keep aloof!

*Patti bursts into the scene.*

**Patti** Cup of tea?

**Kemble** Is that her line?

**Arthur** Not for two pages.

**Patti** I thought I could come on now.

**Kemble** A cup of tea? Someone tell her we're in medieval fucking Germany.

**Siddons** Whenever it's set it becomes the present for the audience.

**Charles** Padua, Illyria, Bethnal Green.

**Mrs Larpent** She was so caught up in the play that she believed it was really happening. How wonderful. Or is it disturbing?

**Patti**  I felt this urge.

**Mrs Larpent**  An urge?

**Siddons**  The worst sort of play leaves you cold and unmoving.

**Charles**  The dead-fish play.

**Patti**  I felt if I didn't do something I'd burst.

**Mrs Larpent**  Burst? In what fashion?

**Kemble**  The wretched play's infected the balance of her mind.

**Mrs Larpent**  Is this true?

**Siddons**  It shows the play has dramatic power. Shall we continue?

**Mrs Larpent**  Say more.

**Patti**  I thought, I'll take on this cup and if that doesn't work I'll do something with the spoon.

**Mrs Larpent**  The spoon? That's irregular.

**Charles**  Out, vile jellies.

**Patti**  Time slowed down, a beating in my ears, my blood, I think, so loud.

**Mrs Larpent**  There is something in this play. I always suspected it.

**Siddons**  A certain female power, Anna, of which we approve.

**Mrs Larpent**  Napoleon, that wretched homunculus, is just over the water. We have to trust our men after all. I need time to think before my husband delivers his final verdict.

**Kemble**  We trust his judgement.

*She goes to exit.*

**Siddons** Anna! Wait!

*She exits.*

**Kemble** Like letting the patient watch their own surgery. It scares them.

**Charles** Well are we on or off? Just when I've learnt my lines. Do I have an actual job?

**Kemble** Wasting our time, we could have been doing one of the Bard's. Packing the house out.

**Siddons** She will stand by me. She's finding her courage to make the right decision.

**Kemble** Curtain up in five hours. It's a disaster. It couldn't be worse if we'd burnt down.

**Siddons** Siddons thinks on her feet. I think we must now take a tea break.

*They break.*

### SIX

*Dressing room.*

**Siddons** What possessed you?

**Patti** I don't know. He was –

**Siddons** Acting. You've jeopardised everything.

**Patti** Sorry. I didn't mean to. It's just . . .

**Siddons** You're not here to do anything interesting. You're a servant.

*Thomas enters.*

**Thomas** Siddons.

**Patti** We told you before you're top of the list.

76

**Siddons**  Why aren't you locked up?

**Thomas**  You wanted me? I'm here.

**Siddons**  Nothing but the direst necessity would force me to engage you. Paint me a new portrait.

**Thomas**  Wounded mother or tragic muse.

**Siddons**  Orra is different.

**Thomas**  Interesting.

**Siddons**  Like nothing that's ever been seen before. No portrait of me you've ever painted.

**Thomas**  My interest is piqued.

**Siddons**  Pique it some more. Patti, the skull.

**Thomas**  Show me.

*Patti gives her the skull.*
    *Siddons transforms herself into the final incarnation of Orra before him.*

**Patti**  She's Orra.

**Thomas**  Can she speak to me?

**Siddons**  Little man, I see through you like a shower of weak piss.

**Thomas**  Fiery isn't she?

**Siddons**  The whole of my sex rages through my words and turns men pale.

**Thomas**  I think I've got her. She wears orange. You need me.

**Siddons**  You need me more.

**Thomas**  Let's agree we are bound together on a wheel of fire.

**Siddons**  I'd be happy watching you burn.

**Thomas** Dear Siddons. In other news I'm getting married.

**Siddons** You quintessence of dust.

**Thomas** I like it. Orra the goddess incarnate. Her hair flowing wildly like an unruly river swelling, bursting its banks.

*Thomas comes close to model her. It could appear as intimacy.*
*Cowslip enters.*

**Cowslip** Oh my days.

**Siddons** This is Mr Lawrence.

**Thomas** I'm painting her portrait. Good day.

*Thomas exits.*

**Cowslip** So we must play the game of strict virtue but you have not played it!

**Patti** She just pushed past me.

**Siddons** When will you learn that sometimes brute force is required.
(*To Cowslip.*) Get out.

*Kemble enters with Scraggs.*

**Kemble** There's an unwholesome crowd gathering. The audience. We don't even know if we've got a play for them. Isn't this supposed to be a theatre?
Here's the ringleader. Mr Scraggs. He has a complaint. Do you know him?

**Siddons** He's a mediocrity, blessedly released from *Hamlet* due to a blow to his metatarsals.

**Scraggs** I trained under Mr Garrick!

**Kemble** Well he's got a talent for troublemaking. Tell her.

**Scraggs** She was to do a benefit for me and she let me down.

**Cowslip** Very noble *on*stage I'm sure.

**Kemble** Who's this?

**Cowslip** 'Cowslip I be, I have the finest bowl of cream this side of the Cotswolds.'

**Kemble** Right.

**Scraggs** All the flyers were up for the Scottish play and I was obliged to make payments for inconvenience.

**Siddons** My daughter was dying.
    In other circumstances I would have obliged.

**Scraggs** Too busy gallivanting with Galindo.

**Cowslip** And now with Mr Lawrence. The famous society portrait painter and well-known Lothario.

**Scraggs** That's news.

**Siddons** Amateurs!

**Kemble** Scraggs, let's find some satisfactory terms. I'll see if I can't dig you out of this hole, sister.

**Scraggs** A benefit or nothing.

**Cowslip** I would like to refuse your terms also.

**Siddons** Do I care?

*They exit. We hear the noise of a crowd.*

What am I, a money pit? Scraggs isn't fit to wipe my –

*Clara enters.*

**Patti** Sir, remove yourself.

**Clara** It's me, Clara.

**Siddons** Clara!

**Clara** I've escaped. On your advice.

**Siddons** You misunderstood me.

**Clara** I acted. Seduced a guard. Knocked his head against the flags. Took his clothes, his money, knife. Here I am. I was going to wait for the slow pace of public opinion to shift over decades but I thought damn it, the kids will have grown up by then.

**Siddons** You can't stay here.

**Clara** I'm not going anywhere.

**Siddons** If you were discovered!

**Clara** I want to see the play *Orra*, you telling my story to the world. How I've been locked up and called mad while my husband steals my money. He's a theatre-goer. I'd like to see his fucking face when he has to watch that baby. Like Claudius watching *The Mousetrap*.

**Siddons** Clara, you've got to help me. Your mother has doubts about the play.

**Clara** Mother must be persuaded.

**Siddons** Conceal yourself until she arrives. We will work on her together.

*Kemble enters with Mrs Larpent and Boaden.*

**Kemble** The crowd out there is fucking enormous.

**Mrs Larpent** Apprentices and tarts. The very worst sort of audience.

**Boaden** None of your upholstery will be safe.

**Kemble** They could burn us to the ground. They've done it before.

**Boaden** Twice.

**Mrs Larpent** Percy Scraggs is leading the chants. A creature called Cowslip is imitating you with a sizeable muff.

**Siddons** What are they saying?

80

**Boaden** 'Siddons is a selfish, mercenary whore.'

**Siddons** Brutes!

**Kemble** They've got the 'whore' bit wrong.

**Siddons** They don't deserve me.

**Patti** How dare they?

**Kemble** They want Scraggs to be recompensed. Someone must go out there and reason with them.

**All** That should be you.

**Kemble** But they don't like me.

**Boaden** Give it a go, man. Courage! I'll wait in the wings to spur you on.

**Kemble** I've got this.

*Kemble and Boaden exit.*

**Mrs Larpent** The revolution. Where will it end?
   Theatre is a dangerous place. Once emotions are let out of their prison they hang about miasmically.

**Siddons** Calm yourself.

**Mrs Larpent** The natural dignity you bring to the stage helps defuse such emissions.
   My dear Sarah, should you play this angry madwoman, I fear for you, for all of us feeling with you. The cobblestones of Paris ran with blood.

**Siddons** I'll go mad if I have to play any more milksops.

**Mrs Larpent** One can always adapt a little more. I always liken myself to the hairy bittercress which negotiates the tiny cracks in the rocks so as to thrive in the sun.

**Siddons** You're comparing yourself to a weed, Anna.
   I feel this part inside me, here.

81

*She grabs Mrs Larpent's hand and places in on her abdomen.*

Like a child.

**Mrs Larpent** Oh Sarah.

**Siddons** Tell him yes.

**Mrs Larpent** It's so very hard to say no to you. I fell in love with your first performance of Queen Katherine when you turned on Cardinal Wolsey – 'You, sir, I'm talking to you' – and the whole court turned and listened. I wept.

**Siddons** Because you do all the work and your husband gets all the credit for it.

**Mrs Larpent** What a thing to say. Out loud. What a dilemma. I need my smelling salts.

**Siddons** No you don't.

**Mrs Larpent** You're right. I only employ them as a prop. Your compelling eyes see straight through me.

**Siddons** I want you to imagine something, Anna.

**Mrs Larpent** I don't really have an imagination. What's the point?

**Siddons** Two women, at the top of their game, who join forces to change the face of British theatre?

**Mrs Larpent** Two women – you mean – like us?

**Siddons** Yes. Must I be consigned with all my lands and rights into the hands of some proud man and say 'Take all, I pray, and do me in return the grace and favour to be my master'?

**Mrs Larpent** It sounds so good in your mouth.

**Siddons** Give me the licence.

**Mrs Larpent**  I must resist. All right. Yes.

**Siddons**  Yes.

> *Mrs Larpent kisses Siddons.*
> *Enter Clara, still disguised as a young man.*

**Clara**  Mother!

**Mrs Larpent**  One of the rioters, come to run us through.

**Clara**  Mother, it's me.

**Mrs Larpent**  Clara! My poor child. I don't know what came over me.

**Clara**  Mother, you're right. *Orra* must be performed. It's my story too. I've been locked up and sent mad. When the world sees it I will be free and my husband will be punished.

**Mrs Larpent**  Clara, your mind is unhinged. To imagine the theatre has any real power. It's all lights and stardust.

**Clara**  I'm not unhinged.

**Mrs Larpent**  You're wearing trousers.

> *A roar from outside is heard as Kemble and Boaden re-enter.*

**Kemble**  Well that worked. They threatened to hang me with my own intestines.
For a performer that's not sustainable. They said I was boring.

**Boaden**  In fairness I think they were only referring to your Hamlet.
Who's this?

**Mrs Larpent**  Mr Boaden, this is my unhappily married daughter the cross-dresser.
She's escaped the asylum and made a bid for freedom due to the play *Orra*, which hasn't even opened.

**Boaden**  This is singular. We have often asked ourselves what precisely is the theatre for? Does it do anything? And here we have a living experiment.

She appears to be unduly influenced by the play's seductions.

**Clara**  Good.

**Siddons**  What's the point of doing a play if you don't think it might change something?

**Boaden**  Careful. There's a mob out there, we don't want to give them dangerous ideas. I'm an expert, I can handle ideas. They could go crazy.

**Mrs Larpent**  Imagine the potential carnage should Orra actually stalk the boards.

**Patti**  You can't blame Orra for what's done to her.

**Siddons**  Anna, remember our pact, don't waver now!

**Clara**  Give her the licence.

**Siddons**  Say something, brother. The world deserves to see your Rudigere.

**Kemble**  It's a tough one. You have overstepped your place, sister. We've got a riot on our hands and all because you wanted your own way.

**Boaden**  Give them traditional fare, the Scottish play, not a new-fangled woman's tragedy.

**Mrs Larpent**  Clara. Come with me.

Your husband is concerned for your welfare, you must return to the madhouse.

**Kemble**  Yes, run along.

**Clara**  No, Mother. I've had a lot of time to think in the madhouse. It's not me that needs to change, it's the law that allows my husband power over me.

**Boaden** Her mind is o'erthrown.

**Clara** I won't be locked up again.

**Mrs Larpent** Assist me, friends.

*The men go to help Mrs Larpent to escort Clara.*
*Siddons steps forward.*

**Siddons** (*as Orra*) Stand back, you fools. Thy rule is fleeting, your resting place will be the grave. Yours is no everlasting power.

**Kemble** She's quoting.

**Boaden** Very good though. I shall regret not seeing it.

**Mrs Larpent** The play is seditious.

**Kemble** And it doesn't even rhyme.

*Siddons flashes the skull at them.*

**Siddons** Run, Clara!

**Clara** Yes. I'll seek my fortune. One day I'll see my babies again.
My God! I can do what I want!
My life is in my own hands. Freedom. It's terrifyingly wonderful.

**Siddons** Tell me how it feels? Exactly.

**Clara** Like you've given birth in a great big bloody rush and your hot new child is put into your arms and you feel so strong, so magnificent, you could leap from the window, fly.

*Clara takes out her dagger and keeps them at bay and exits.*

**Siddons** Fly!

**Mrs Larpent** Fly, child. I never said that.
What I meant to say was Clara must be hunted down and returned to domesticity. This is your doing, Siddons.

It's the role of a censor to hold back any material from the public that might encourage free expression. I was tricked because it was set in Germany. My God, I could lose my husband's job. I retract the licence for *Orra*. My husband's decision is final.

**Siddons** Too late, the audience has gathered.

**Mrs Larpent** You perform *Orra* at your peril.

**Kemble** Peril, sister. Cancel it. The theatre will have to take the hit.

**Boaden** You are besieged on every front – the theatre threatened with destruction – the censor at your throat. That your biographer is here to witness it all is miraculous.

**Kemble** The almighty scandal of all scandals.

**Siddons** Siddons draws herself to her full height and turns to face her accusers. If she cannot do *Orra* then she will never act again.

**Patti** And I won't either. Work backstage I mean.

*A huge roar from the crowd.*

**Mrs Larpent** You have separated a mother from her children!

**Boaden** My dear Siddons. Think of your reputation.

**Kemble** The fines.

**Mrs Larpent** You will be known henceforth as the scourge of mothers.

**Siddons** The scourge of mothers?

**Boaden** A lifetime of success only to burn out like a dead star in the end?

**Kemble** The longest partnership of my life. Don't turn your back on me. Sister.

**Siddons** Tell your husband the play *Orra* is to be let go.

**Patti** No.

**Mrs Larpent** I'll tell him his decision immediately.

*Mrs Larpent exits.*
*Another roar heard, crashing.*

**Kemble** I won't go back out there. It's a pit of snakes. My legs won't go in the same direction.

**Siddons** Useful detail.

**Kemble** Not everything's about fucking acting.

**Siddons** Of course it is. You elf-skin.

**Boaden** They want Siddons. To say she will do a benefit for Scraggs.

**Siddons** I know what they want.

*Siddons comes to the front of the stage.*
*Booing.*
*Hoots.*

Friends. You who have been my constant companions have been woefully misinformed.

*Jeers.*

I feel for the suffering of Scraggs and his family as only a mother can, of course I do. The night's proceedings are all for them.

*Jeers.*

Dear Mr Scraggs who had the misfortune to have three toes crushed while attempting to act.

*Jeers.*

I'm a woman of my word. Please put down your potatoes.

*She changes tack and is demanding not pleading.*
*Crowd quiets.*

If you desire to watch me perform, then you will do me the honour of refraining from arson. If you do not wish to see me perform, I shall retire. Forever.

*Gasps and cries.*
*Quietness.*

Have I your permission to do what I do best?

*Shouts of 'Yes!'*

We will perform the Scottish play tonight.

SEVEN

*The dressing room.*
*Patti, Siddons. Joanna. Joanna carries a card.*

**Joanna** It's happened again? That's not possible?

**Siddons** It just hasn't worked out this time.

**Joanna** In my mind she's alive. Orra.

**Siddons** A little ahead of your time perhaps.

**Joanna** You begged me to write you a play and I did. You can't slam the door in my face now.

**Siddons** We're sorry.

**Joanna** This is my only chance, otherwise I'm just a person who tried to get their plays on their whole life and never did. First-night card. (*She scrumples it up.*)
The stranger inside. Well, now we know yours.

**Siddons** Siddons waits for the punchline.

**Joanna** A traitor. To yourself, I meant.

*Joanna exits.*

**Patti** I'm saying goodbye too, going home.

**Siddons** No you're not, Patti, I need you here with me.

**Patti** Rudigere tries to take Orra's honour.
   The play shows what it's like – how you freeze up. And after there's just this big awful silence and you have to hold all the broken bits of you together and you're always frightened you're going to drop them or that it's changed you and you'll never know who you'd have been if it never happened. Even if it didn't quite happen.

**Siddons** You have put a lot of thought into it, Patti. Don't go imagining that marriage is vastly different.

**Patti** People can seem special onstage but they're just ordinary. Goodbye.

*Patti turns to go.*

**Siddons** Wait. Here.

*She takes off her locket, gives it to Patti.*
*Patti exits.*


### EIGHT

**Siddons** Drury Lane Theatre, 1800. Enter Siddons, statuesque, dark eyes, dark hair, she moves like a woman of superior rank. She begins preparations. For the Scottish Queen.

*Siddons transforms into Lady Macbeth.*

## NINE

*We are onstage.*

*Dark, thunderous, threatening.*

*From out of the gloom emerges Siddons as the dreadful incarnation of Lady Macbeth. Throughout this scene we hear the audience respond. Siddons's performance is the most powerful and forbidding she has ever done, and as the scene progresses it unnerves Kemble.*

*We join them mid-scene.*

**Kemble** (*as Macbeth, looking at his hands*)
This is a sorry sight.

**Siddons** (*as Lady Macbeth*)
A foolish thought, to say 'a sorry sight'.

**Kemble** (*as Macbeth*)
There's one did laugh in's sleep, and one cried 'Murder!'
That they did wake each other: I stood and heard them.
But they did say their prayers, and addressed them
Again to sleep.

**Siddons** (*as Lady Macbeth*)
There are two lodged together.

**Kemble** (*as Macbeth*)
One cried 'God bless us' and 'Amen' the other,
As they had seen me with these hangman's hands.
List'ning their fear, I could not say 'Amen',
When they did say 'God bless us.'

**Siddons** (*as Lady Macbeth*)
Consider it not so deeply.

**Kemble** (*as Macbeth*)
But wherefore could not I pronounce 'Amen'?
I had most need of blessing, and 'Amen'
Stuck in my throat.

**Siddons**  (*as Lady Macbeth*)
>These deeds must not be thought
>After these ways: so, it will make us mad.

>*Something about the way she says the word 'mad' alerts*
>*Kemble.*
>>*And unnerves him.*

**Kemble**  (*as Macbeth*)
>Methought I heard a voice cry 'Sleep no more,
>Macbeth does murder sleep: the innocent sleep' –

>*She cuts him off. This also jolts him.*

**Siddons**  (*as Lady Macbeth*)
>What do you mean?

**Kemble**  (*as Macbeth*)
>Still it cried 'Sleep no more' to all the house:
>'Glamis hath murdered sleep, and therefore Cawdor
>Shall sleep no more, Macbeth shall sleep no more.'

**Siddons**  (*as Lady Macbeth*)
>Who was it that thus cried? Why, worthy thane,
>You do unbend your noble strength to think
>So brainsickly of things. Go get some water
>And wash this filthy witness from your hand.

>*At this point, Siddons becomes overbearing in the*
>*extreme and worries Kemble even more.*

>Why did you bring these daggers from the place?
>They must lie there: go carry them and smear
>The sleepy grooms with blood.

**Kemble**  (*as Macbeth*)
>I'll go no more
>I am afraid to think what I have done:
>Look on't again I dare not.

>*Siddons looms over Kemble; he shrinks, terrified now.*

**Siddons** (*as Lady Macbeth*)
Infirm of purpose!
Give me the daggers!

*She grabs them from him.*
   *She approaches him closely with a dagger waving close to his face/chest.*
   *Vocals from the audience.*

The sleeping and the dead
Are but as pictures: 'tis the eye of childhood
That fears a painted devil. If he do bleed –

*At this point she cuts into Macbeth's costume with her dagger.*

**Kemble** Aaagh!

**Siddons** (*as Lady Macbeth*)
I'll gild the faces of the grooms withal –

*She wipes the daggers on his face.*
   *Gasps from audience.*

For it must seem their guilt.

*She stands as if possessed.*
   *Kemble whispers to her.*

**Kemble** Get off me, sister, off. Get off!

*She comes to, and exits. He exits.*
   *Kemble is on the sofa in her dressing room.*
   *Siddons is sponging the blood on his chest.*

Did you have to draw blood? You crossed a line.

**Siddons** It wasn't me, it was her.

**Kemble** She's a character! Words on a page don't cut you open.
   You are too masculine, sister, how can I be expected to act beside you? Ranting and towering over me – he's

supposed to be a fucking general. You make Macbeth look a ninny. You're unnatural.

**Siddons** Perhaps, but I can't help the way I am.

**Kemble** I'm going to faint.

*Siddons throws some water at him.*

Thanks. It's a miracle I staggered through the banquet scene.

**Siddons** Just the last act to go.

**Kemble** I was in the park the other day and I passed a group chatting. 'Kemble is a fine tragic actor despite a tendency to obscure diction.' And they all agreed. And I swear I was infused with happiness. Then a woman said, 'Surpassed by his sister, Siddons, she dwarfs him.' And they all agreed 'of course', naturally, she's a goddess.

**Siddons** Eavesdroppers rarely hear good things.

**Kemble** I wasn't eavesdropping, I was walking in the fucking park. You're everywhere. I can't get away from you.

**Siddons** Has it made me happy?

**Kemble** Ecstatic I imagine.

**Siddons** You can't blame me, brother.

**Kemble** Charisma – the breath of a God. You have it and I don't.

**Siddons** I didn't ask for it.

**Kemble** It was a mistake. It should have been mine. We're not on together any more. Thank God. You just have to go mad.

**Siddons** Yes.

**Kemble** That was the best I've ever seen you do it, by the way. You were just lucky it wasn't an eye.

*He gets up.*

**Siddons** It was the best you've ever done it too.

**Kemble** Really?

**Siddons** You connected with the fear. When I stabbed you.

**Kemble** Yes. I was pretty damn good. Of course the wisdom of the ancients tell us all these God-given gifts are double-edged. Half curse. That force in you. Too much inside.
　And you're right about the soppy parts. You're too old for them anyway.

**Siddons** An actress can play any age. I can play twenty-five. I can play Lear.

**Kemble** It's going to be hard for you when it's over.

**Siddons** It's not over. I'd make a better Lear.

**Kemble** The audience requires me.

　*He exits.*
　　*We hear echoes of the play offstage.*
　　*She listens.*
　　*Patti enters with a travelling bag.*

**Siddons** Patti. Are you married?

**Patti** No. I was on my way and I started to think. Weighed up being married to Dicky or working here and I thought I prefer to work. I'm good at my job. So I got off at the first stop and caught the next coach back.

**Siddons** Well done. Don't say I said that, Patti.

**Patti** On the way back to London our coach was robbed.

**Siddons** Are you hurt?

**Patti** No. Everyone was saying it was the politest robbery they'd ever had.

He stopped me and said, 'Here, Patti – I won't take your locket.' He gave it back to me.

**Siddons**  How unusual.

**Patti**  The highwayman, it was Clara.
   She gave me one of her pistols. She stole them from props on the way out. I'll show it to Mr Kemble. Just once. A glimpse.

*She reveals a glimpse of the pistol.*

Just so he knows where I stand. You'll need to be going on.

**Siddons**  Tonight the lady came very strongly. She was raging and I pierced my brother's flesh.

**Patti**  Thanks. Time.

**Siddons**  Drury Lane Theatre. Enter Siddons, statuesque, dark hair, dark eyes, moves like a woman of superior rank.

*Patti begins to help her get ready.*

'How now you secret black and midnight hags.'
   Though he'll say ''aaaags'.

**Patti**  Yes he will.

**Siddons**  Siddons prepares to go on. Stray thoughts, fractious children. Over? Think bloody hands. Siddons pulls herself together. Siddons must clear her mind.
   Bloody hands. Weight of conscience. Great wheel of fortune ready to drag her down. Too much inside?
   Clear your mind. Siddons prepares to go on. Bloody hands. Kemble will get Lear! They'd never let me stumble about with a beard. Howl howl howl. That's how to go mad, raging, thundering. Not wringing your hands, finishing it all offstage. Siddons prepares to go on. So many parts. Seventeen in my head and then there's home. An old actor in my father's company became terrified he was going to step off the stage, fall, break his neck. Got worse and

worse till he refused to walk downstage at all, had to be released. He cried 'Where will I go?' You have to keep taking the next step forward. Over? There is nothing beneath my feet.

Clear your mind. Fingers on lips. Smile, move in a regal manner. Siddons prepares to go on.

I made her with you. (*She gestures to audience.*) Our pact to see me suffering, broken. It reassures you. I can't exercise control over you and survive. The world would turn upside down. With all this inside! A revolution. Howl. Howl. Howl.

**Patti** Stop. Go out and go mad, not in here.

**Siddons** Where's the candle?

**Patti** Here. They love you.

**Siddons** Dear Egg. Siddons steps from the wings and into the light.

*We see Siddons approach the audience, extraordinary intensity. She comes forward with a candle. Deafening applause which Siddons responds to, coming alive until darkness swallows her.*

*End.*